Peter Schreiner, Friedhelm Kraft, Andr

Good Practice in Religious Educa

Schriften aus dem Comenius-Institut

herausgegeben von

Volker Elsenbast

Band 15

LIT

Peter Schreiner, Friedhelm Kraft, Andrew Wright (Eds.)

Good Practice
in Religious Education in Europe

Examples and Perspectives of Primary Schools

LIT

Cover Picture: Dietlind Fischer, Münster

Bibliographic information published by the Deutsche Nationalbibliothek
The Deutsche Nationalbibliothek lists this publication in the Deutsche
Nationalbibliografie; detailed bibliographic data are available in the Internet at
http://dnb.d-nb.de.

ISBN 978-3-8258-9076-6

A catalogue record for this book is available from the British Library

© LIT VERLAG Dr. W. Hopf Berlin 2007
Chausseestr. 128 – 129
D-10115 Berlin

Auslieferung:
LIT Verlag Fresnostr. 2, D-48159 Münster
Tel. +49 (0) 2 51/620 32 - 22, Fax +49 (0) 2 51/922 60 99, e-Mail: lit@lit-verlag.de

Distributed in the UK by: Global Book Marketing, 99B Wallis Rd, London, E9 5LN
Phone: +44 (0) 20 8533 5800 – Fax: +44 (0) 1600 775 663
http://www.centralbooks.co.uk/acatalog/search.html

Distributed in North America by:

Transaction Publishers
New Brunswick (U.S.A.) and London (U.K.)

Transaction Publishers
Rutgers University
35 Berrue Circle
Piscataway, NJ 08854

Phone: +1 (732) 445 - 2280
Fax: + 1 (732) 445 - 3138
for orders (U. S. only):
toll free (888) 999 - 6778
e-mail:
orders@transactionspub.com

Contents

Contents

Acknowledgements

Producing a book in the context of Europe today is an exciting exercise. Nevertheless, those who direct the project, together with the experts and enthusiasts involved in the process, need perseverance and creativity.

Special thanks go first of all to the authors, drawn from different countries of Europe. From the context in which they work, they have been courageous enough to describe what they see as good practice in religious education, while aiming to share elements of their work as well as their understanding about teaching and learning in RE. In December 2005, we were able to meet for a seminar involving intensive exchange of ideas at the Protestant University of Education in Berlin with financial support from the RE Centre in Loccum. The seminar encouraged contributors to engage in deeper dialogue and to sharpen the profile of their individual contributions.

A European project has also to be sensitive to the issue of language. We are indebted to Gaynor Pollard, James Barnett and Volker Bach who provided linguistic support for the non English writers.

The project has gained much from the involvement of Dr. William James, currently working at Bangor University, who set the pace for the initiative when he was still working at King's College, London.

Angelika Boekestein from the Comenius-Institut organised the manuscript with the self-evident professionalism for which she is known. Our thanks go to Angelika for her patience and flexibility in the careful handling of different drafts of the text.

We also thank the Comenius-Institut both for accepting the project and for the subsequent support that lead to its publication. The LIT Verlag in Münster agreed, without hesitation, to publish the book as part of the 'Comenius-Institut' series. We are grateful to Dr. Michael J. Rainer for all his support and encouragement.

We dedicate this book to RE teachers in Europe who – in different contexts – support the spiritual and religious development of pupils and students through their sensitive and empathetic approach to teaching and learning.

Münster, London, Loccum, February 2007

Peter Schreiner, Friedhelm Kraft, Andrew Wright

Introduction

Peter Schreiner

The *Good Practice in Religious Education in Primary Schools in Europe Project* aims to identify and disseminate examples of successful and innovative classroom practice to religious education by teachers across Europe. Herewith we present case studies from different countries designed to enhance the work of primary religious education teachers across Europe by providing them with models of good practice.

The project acknowledges the importance of religious education in the classrooms of European schools. As an important subject in all of the represented countries religious education contributes to learning about religions that focus on knowledge and understanding of religions and beliefs in the world today and learning from religions that offers students opportunities for personal reflection and spiritual development developing their own focus and also to learning through religions that brings these aims together in a more integrated way according to different approaches to religious education in the countries.

It also underlines the relation between religious education, the wider curriculum and whole school initiatives. Increasingly an integrated perspective is being adopted when it comes to the development of schooling and its respective structures and concepts.

Background and Development

The project originated in 2003, following discussions between the Comenius-Institut, Münster, the Protestant Applied University for Education, Berlin, and King's College, London. A detailed project plan was drawn up between the coordinators of the project. Extensive consultations with a number of European religious educators then led to the identification of a range of case studies of good practice in primary religious education. Potential contributors were invited to draft an initial account of their work, following guidelines supplied by the project directors. The entire project team met for a seminar in autumn 2004 in Berlin, to discuss the case studies and revise the draft contributions. Following that meeting, the contributors submitted final drafts following dialogue with each other and with the editors of this book. So the process has been one of experience, dialogue and collaboration across Europe.

Aims and Scope

The project aims to identify and publish case studies of good practice in primary religious education across a range of European countries.

Each case study focuses directly on successful and innovative primary level classroom practice. Contributors have outlined the strengths of their classroom pedagogy, contrasting it with examples of bad practice. Reference is made to the theory supporting the classroom practice, and also to the nature of the participation of both pupils and teachers. Each contributor was guided by a series of key questions:

– How does the practice link up with the life-worlds of the pupils?
– How is the teaching linked to specific religious traditions?
– What are the pedagogical principles underlying the teaching and learning that takes place?
– How does the teaching relate to the mainstream of existing teaching methods in religious education?
– How does the practice link to the overall mission of the school?

The project's aims was not to promote a 'European model for primary RE teaching.' This would ignore the richness of diversity among religious education in Europe, the different contexts and the different histories. Instead, the project contributes to a vivid debate about how religious education should be organised to support the spiritual development of children across Europe.

The project does not ignore that religious education is a contested area in the education systems across Europe due to the existing diversity of traditions and approaches.

Therefore this introductory article provides a broader picture of the debate on religious education in Europe. It argues that however much approaches may differ, a tendency towards good practice in RE that meets the need of the pupils can be observed across Europe.

The primary level of education

Primary education, sometimes called elementary education, refers to educational programs that are normally designed on a unit or project basis to give pupils between the ages of 4 and 12 a sound basic education in reading, writing and mathematics along with an elementary understanding of other subjects such as history, geography, natural science, social science, art and music. In most countries in Europe religious education is also featured. These subjects serve to develop pupils' abilities to obtain and use necessary information about their home, community, country, etc.

The project has brought together scholars from different contexts in which primary education shows significant national variation, e.g. in the entrance age of children or in the amount of time children spend in school. In some countries children start in year 4 with primary education (e.g. Netherlands) in others in year six (e.g Germany, Bulgaria, Norway) or even in year 7 (e.g. Estonia, Finland). Also, where in some countries primary education is organised as a separate stage of education, in others it forms part of an integrated school system. Consequently, we have asked the authors to introduce basic information about their national education system in their articles.

We have also discussed what we understand by 'Good Practice'. No common understanding can be reported because as contexts differ, so does the understanding of 'Good Practice'. Nevertheless, a common feature that helped us to evaluate examples of good practice could be identified. In our judgement good practice tended to occur wherever the orientation of teaching and learning towards the situation and the life-world of the child was given prominence. In these classrooms children were seen as active meaning-makers or active meaning-searchers and their dignity was respected. This impacted on the teaching and learning arrangements that can be seen in many of the examples of good practice in this volume.

The wider context: Religious Education in Europe

RE in Europe is grounded in factors that can be seen as different 'layers' of the subject: the religious landscape in the country, the role and value of religion in society, the relation between state and religion, the history, politics and structure of the education system, etc. Each approach to religious education is shaped by a specific composition with different layers.

In general it is possible to differentiate roughly between two main models of RE in Europe: the *Religious Studies approach* and the *Denominational or Confessional approach*. One has to be aware that this simplification can nurture prejudices and stereotypes.

The differentiation between 'denominational' and 'religious studies' refers to the fact that the content of RE, the training and facilitating of teachers, and the development of curricula and teaching material are mainly the responsibility of either religious communities or of the state. In the case of denominationally oriented RE, it must be emphasised that this approach is not necessarily understood as a consequence of the existence of a state church or of a majority religion; rather it is best seen as the expression of the state's neutrality and the individual's freedom of religion. The task of the state is not to influence the contents of the subject, but to be neutral towards religion and worldviews. Where churches and religious communities have a legal say in public education, they see their involvement in education and RE in state maintained schools mainly as a service to society and as a field of close cooperation with the state rather than primarily as a means of nurturing or recruiting church members. Where RE is denominational oriented (e.g.

in southern Europe, parts of Switzerland, Austria, Belgium and Germany, and areas of central and eastern Europe) different kinds of religious education are offered. In Austria, Belgium and parts of Germany denominational religious education is not limited to Catholic or Protestant teaching but it includes also Orthodox, Jewish, Muslim, Buddhist and other forms of religious education. In many cases there is an opportunity for pupils to opt out and to choose alternative subjects such as ethics or philosophy.

Most of the countries with a Religious Studies approach do not have a general right to opt out (e.g. Denmark, Sweden and Norway), others do (e.g. England, Wales and Scotland), and in some countries it is granted to members of religious minorities or for faith oriented phases of the teaching (e.g. Norway). The general aims are to transmit religious knowledge and understanding, as well as dealing with human experiences. The neutrality of the state and the right of religious freedom are reflected in this approach differently from the way that it is expressed in denominational religious education. The religious studies approach is carried out under the authority of the state. Instruction is not to be neutral in respect to values but should be neutral in respect of worldviews including religion, a demand which corresponds to the religious neutrality of the state. From this perspective, this neutrality seeks to guarantee that this kind of religious education is equally acceptable to all denominations and religions.

Different projects have given evidence to the fact that we can no longer be satisfied with existing labels. What confessional or non-confessional means in one country might be significantly different in another country. In one context 'confessional' might be understood as a form of 'indoctrination' that should not be an underlying purpose of any approach to education; in other contexts it might refer to a shared sponsorship of education and/or religious education.[1]

---

1 'Others are more sceptical because they work from the assumption that the combination of the characteristics of 'denominational' and 'educational' can only lead to contradictions. In addition, there is a language problem. In the UK, 'confessional' in the context of religious education is often understood as 'indoctrination'. In Germany, designations like 'denominational' or 'confessional' refer to a sponsorship for religious education that is shared between the state and religious communities. It does not refer to the expected outcome. Even from the point of view of the churches, German denominational religious education does not have the task of turning children or adolescents into followers of a certain religious community or church. Religious education should give them a chance to encounter a clear religious outlook but not in order for them to be indoctrinated. The aim is considered choice – a choice in the sense of what I like to call principled pluralism.' (F. Schweitzer, CoGREE Conference 2005)

Different approaches, different aims?

Different approaches have different aims. The more denominationally oriented RE programmes focus on the 'identity formation' of the pupils with
particular reference to the religious dimension. The articles from Austria,
Bulgaria, Germany, Italy, and the Netherlands are examples of this approach.
The more 'religious studies' oriented approaches are concerned to a greater
extent with knowledge about and understanding of religion. This is exem-
plified in the articles from England & Wales, Northern Ireland and Norway.
In Estonia and Finland the approaches are also non-confessional. Labels like
these are of limited value because they cannot represent the complexity of
each of the national or regional approaches. So one should be careful not to
overload these labels but try to find out what happens in the classroom.

Looking to the different RE classrooms in Europe, it can be argued that
there is a tendency for practice to converge despite the presence of different
'theories'. This can be observed in an increasing awareness of the relation of
religion to the pupils, their own individual religious practice and their 'religious needs'. This view includes recognition of the need to match the capacity of the students to comprehend religious issues with the presentation of a
dynamic understanding of religion.

A comparison of the aims of religious education in different national
contexts (Schreiner 1999; 2002) reveals similarities. For example many cata-
logues of aims of RE include:
- to encourage pupils to be sensitive to religion and the religious dimension of life;
- to provide orientation towards the variety of existing religious possibilities and ethical understandings which are rooted in religious experiences;
- to give knowledge and understanding of religious beliefs and experiences.

Reasons for this convergence may include a central awareness of religious
education as a pedagogical enterprise and an increasing awareness of the attitudes and day-to-day experiences of the pupil.

This change of perspective includes a different understanding of religion
and culture. Both are seen as dynamic interwoven areas with every definition
having no more than a preliminary status. There is no religion or culture that
has not changed in history: more emphasis is given to the concrete 'gestalt' of
religion with each individual. A change in the perception of religion from an
institutionalised tradition to personal aspects of believers, and the acceptance
of the 'Children's right to religion' (Schweitzer, 2000) could become a new
stimulus for pan-European debate concerning RE. The orientation of education, the orientation towards the attitudes and the experiences of the pupils
can also provide stimulus to the debate on the existing approaches to RE.

Speaking about 'biographies' of religious education in Europe can encourage a careful consideration of and readiness to explore different understandings of RE. It can sharpen one's own view about RE and provide opportunities for dialogue among RE practitioners and scholars without nurturing the development of a single European approach to RE, which would inevitably ignore the richness of cultures and religions in Europe. Conversely it should not hinder any discussion of some common or specific challenges to RE.

Challenges

All approaches are challenged by radical changes in society. Issues such as secularisation, individualism, pluralism, and globalisation are markers of changes which influence the field of religious education. In most of the western European countries the emergence of modernity coincided with the secularisation of society. The idea behind the 'secularisation thesis' is quite simple: modernisation leads to a decline of religion, both in society and in the minds of individuals. However there are good arguments to support the view expressed in 'De-secularisation of the World' (Berger, 1999) that the relation between religion and modernity is complex, and the fact that 'certain religious institutions have lost power and influence in many societies' does not mean that religious belief and spiritual sensibility is on the decline (Berger, 1999:3). One consequence of this is the trend for religion to become more individualised. 'Religion, like so many other things, has entered the world of options, life-styles, and preferences' (Davie, 1999:75). We have to be aware of the situation of plurality which means that European societies are characterised by the presence of different political attitudes, cultural backgrounds, ethnic identifications, religious convictions, and worldviews.

These developments have consequences for RE. The existing *denominational approach* can no longer focus exclusively in one specific faith tradition. A much stronger emphasis is needed on ecumenical and inter-religious learning for the sake of mutual understanding and the promotion of respect towards other faith traditions and world views.

From the very beginning the *religious studies approach* has included a variety of other religions and world views by adopting a comparative approach towards religious phenomena. What appears to be missing here is cooperation with faith communities, associations and organisations which can give authentic testimony to their beliefs and religious views. In a consultation of the World Council of Churches the value of RE in this radical changed situation was underlined:

> In societies where religious indifference, cultural intolerance and rapidly changing norms and values seem to prevail, RE can be the space in which young people learn how to deal with challenges to identity,

manage conflict and develop sensitivity in interacting with difference. The task of conceptualising RE, in dialogue with other faith traditions is an essential way forward. (WCC, 2000:1)

Proponents of any model of RE must be able to demonstrate how it contributes to the following tasks:
- dealing with questions and challenges of identity formation;
- developing ways of handling conflicts;
- encouraging ways of dealing with difference.

This short description makes clear that one cannot separate RE from school and school development, even if the role and place of RE is contested in some education systems. The issues of a religious dimension in general education and of RE in schools seem to be unavoidable in the context of the following questions, which in turn raise challenges for the whole education system:
- How can school contribute to a mutual understanding between the existing cultural and religious traditions and views in society?
- How can religious and ethical education be organised appropriately in order to deal with the existing plurality in society?

In this respect RE can become an important factor in the general debate about education but it must demonstrate its ability to respond to conflicting expectations such as:
- *Society* expects that RE should act as a problem-solver for conflicts in society contributing to the peaceful cohabitation of people with different cultural and religious backgrounds.
- *Parents* expect that school will provide a religious education which they cannot or will not provide for their children at home.
- *Religious communities* expect that the way religious traditions are presented in RE will be authentic and in coherence with their self understanding, leading to the question 'Who represents the religion(s) in the classroom?' answers to which can lead to the situation where RE is confused with catechetics and religious instruction, a task best left to the religious communities themselves when educating their members.
- *Politicians* expect RE to reflect and induct students into the inherent ethical potential of religion.

However, education and religious education cannot be seen as magic healers for problems and conflicts which are rooted in other areas of society. For religious educators it is a charming but nevertheless dangerous temptation when politicians claim religious education can and should solve existing problems of living together in Europe.

'Europeanisation' of RE?

The introduction so far shows that religious education in Europe is rooted in a specific and complex situation in each country, and that all existing RE approaches are challenged by recent developments in society and in Europe. In a book about good practice in RE in Europe it is worth asking: How can we compare the different approaches to RE and is there a tendency to 'Europeanisation'? Confirming the need and benefit of international exchange and co-operation in RE, we should be aware of existing obstacles and problems which can be experienced at any European conference on religious education and also during the process of our project:

- *The problem of terminology.* What do we understand when we talk about Religious Education? A common starting point could be that we deal with a school subject as part of a general school curriculum. But then we soon recognise that the term RE is embedded in a specific context with different starting points, backgrounds and histories. Are we sensitive to these differences? Are we open for other than our own views? It seems to me that it is better to dance with the differences than to ignore them.
- *The problem of language and culture barriers* that lie between many of the European countries. In most of the cases the linguistic communities correspond to cultural communities shaped by a common history. Language is a mirror and tool of culture and different languages carry different bags of culture. There is no other approach than to find ways of dealing with these existing barriers. Crossing boundaries can be a fruitful experience.
- *The differences in the existing education systems.* Religious Education depends not least on the frame and the structure of the education system. In any society the right of the parents to be responsible for the education of their children as well as the right of religious communities for authentic self-interpretation are decisive criteria for RE. The debate about the role, place and value of RE is an ongoing process for the sake of facilitating religious competence of the pupils and young adults. It is a debate about good education where the religious dimension must not be ignored.

There is a debate among scholars of RE about international agreement on the basic criteria for what should be considered good quality religious education, especially in terms of the countries within the European Union. Any of such criteria can only be achieved by the way of mutually critical dialogue.

It also makes sense to think about minimum requirements or basic standards for religious education that should be guaranteed in all countries irrespective of their special situation. Schweitzer (2004) has suggested five examples for such standards in respect to RE in schools:

- Religion must and can be taught in line with the criteria of general education (educational quality).
- RE is of relevance to the public and must be taught in line with this relevance (contribution to general education).
- RE must include some aspects of interdenominational and inter-religious learning which are in line with the increasingly pluralist situation in many countries (dialogical quality, contribution to peace and tolerance).
- RE must be based on the children's right to religion and religious education (child-centred approach based on children's rights, cf. Schweitzer, 2000).
- RE teachers must be professionals in the sense that they have reached a level of self-understanding and professional reflection based on academic work which allows for a critical appropriation of their religious backgrounds and biographies (professional teaching).

This clearly is not a complete list but the examples may still be helpful. Among others, they indicate that such criteria, if accepted by an international body of religious education specialists, could give religious educators in different countries a better basis for setting forth their demands within their own national contexts. Similarly, such criteria and requirements could be helpful in the much needed dialogue with the European Union about religious education.

This rough introduction to the discourse on religious education in Europe might help to see the case studies in this book in a larger frame.

The book is structured around discrete case studies from a number of European countries. Each case study will have a similar structure, oriented on three sections:

1. *Overview of education system, primary education and religious education.* This includes dealing with the following areas and questions: The general situation of primary education and the role and place of RE (e.g. taught in a certain time of the day, special teachers, monitor of the syllabus, attempts to integrate RE with other subjects of the curriculum). Who is doing the RE teaching – the classroom teacher, a special teacher? What are the aims of RE in primary school?
2. *Methods and example of good practice.* A case study of a particular classroom-based teaching/learning situation. What methods are preferred? How is the method in the example of good practice linked to the situation of the child? How is the method linked to the religious traditions? What are the pedagogical principles that inform this method? How does the method fit in the mainstream of existing teaching methods in RE? Are there links to the overall mission of the school?
3. *Perspectives.* Reflections on the case studies from participant teachers and contributors.

Each of the case studies gives a special flavour of the context of RE in the specific country. The headings already indicate the main idea of the example of good practice. In Austria the method of a 'learning circuit' has been used successful especially to take into account the different abilities, skills and talents of pupils. A special situation is identified in Bulgaria where the introduction of Orthodox RE is influenced by dynamics of the Orthodox Church in Bulgaria. The issue of how school books should be written is one of the main areas of dispute. The English context in RE is shaped by the variety of different cultural and religious background among the pupils. The 'pupils to pupils dialogue' provides opportunities to encounter in a global context among the different cultures using ICT facilities in a fruitful way. In Estonia and Finland methods of storytelling have gained prominence. In Germany a new approach takes into account that children have skills and competence to deal with theological issues themselves. Therefore 'theologising with children' in the RE classroom is resonated in a positive way by many teachers. Teaching religion through art is the main focus from the example of Italy. Shaped by Roman Catholicism RE is open for all pupils and focus more and more on pedagogical principles and aims. In the Netherlands a great number of schools (2/3 of all schools) are religiously based either from the perspective of a Protestant tradition or from a Catholic one. The good example presented from that context focus on the educational quality of the learning process in RE. For Northern Ireland RE contributes to the attempt to deal in a constructive way with a still segregated society. The term 'enriched RE' represents an approach that provides more opportunities for children to encounter stories, people and places in a more creative and active way. The main focus in Norway nowadays is how to organise RE by taking into account the existing difference in the classroom. A dynamic of school curriculum reform during the last years has focused also on RE and the process continues.

References

Berger, P. L. (1999) (Ed.) *The Desecularization of the World* (Grand Rapids).

Davie G. (1999) 'Europe: The Exception That Proves the Rule?', in: P.L. Berger (Ed.) *The Desecularization of the World* (Grand Rapids), 65-83.

Debray, R. (2002) *L'Enseignement Du Fait Religieux Dans L'École Laïque* (Paris, Odile Jacob).

Schreiner, P. (1999) Different Approaches to RE/RS in European Schools – the Scandinavian Approach in a European Context, in: N.-Å. Tidman (Ed.) *Into the third Millennium... EFTRE conference August 1998 in Copenhagen*, 111-129 (Malmö, FLR).

Schreiner, P. (2002) Religious Education in the European context, in: L. Broadbent & A. Brown (Eds.) *Issues in religious education* (London/New York, Routledge/Falmer), 86-98.

Schweitzer, F. (2000) *Das Recht des Kindes auf Religion [The Children's Right to Religion]* (Gütersloh, Gütersloher Verlagshaus).

Schweitzer, F. (2004) Comparative Research in Religious Education: International-Inter-denominational-Interreligious, in: R. Larsson & C. Gustavsson (Eds.) *Towards a European Perspective on Religious Education* (Skellefteå, Artos & Norma).

Schweitzer, F. (2005) *Education for Peace and Tolerance. New Tasks for Religious Education.* Paper to the CoGREE Conference 2005 in Berlin, CD ROM (Münster 2006).

World Council of Churches (2000) Concepts on Teaching and Learning in Religions, in: *EEF-Net* 6-2000, 10-11.

The Learning Circuit in Religious Education in Austrian Schools

Gerhild Herrgesell and Helmar Pollitt

Introduction

Austria is a relatively small country with a population of eight million, of whom two million live in the capital city Vienna. In a way, Austria today can be seen as the remnant centre of the once large Habsburg Monarchy, which collapsed after the First World War. Conditions in the country between the two wars can be compared to a civil war, and this influenced Austrian politics after the Second World War. Though an awareness of Austrian nationality emerged in the post-war period, deep mistrust between the upper/middle class and the socialist camp influenced the general Austrian perspective on education and educational policy until recently. All legal regulations concerning school-based education required a two-thirds majority in the National Assembly; this made fundamental changes in the education system almost impossible to achieve. However, new approaches could be developed through so-called 'school experiments', which could be introduced by ministerial orders. Over time Austria became a country with many school experiments. In June 2005 the National Assembly rescinded the requirement of a two-thirds majority in the area of education legislation.

The size of Roman Catholic population in Austria has decreased in recent years, and today stands at 75% in the country as a whole and only 50% in Vienna. Protestants make up 5% of the population, while the growing Muslim community now amounts to 4% of the population. All other religious communities have a share of less than 1%.

1. Austrian School System, Primary Schools and Religious Education

The school system in Austria is basically organised by the central government. Apart from the majority of public schools there are a few religiously affiliated schools linked to the Roman Catholic, Protestant, Jewish or Islamic communities. These schools generally follow the state curriculum. There are also a few private schools. Between the ages of six and ten children attend primary school; at the secondary level parents and pupils have a choice between general secondary school (Hauptschule) or upper secondary school (Gymnasium). The Hauptschule takes pupils between the ages of ten and fourteen and covers four school years, while the Gymnasium accepts pupils between the ages of ten and eighteen and covers eight school years. At the end of their time in the Hauptschule, or after four years at the Gymnasium, students have the option of attending specialist schools, which focus on either the start of vocational training or on preparation for the university entrance diploma.

In the nineteenth century religious education (RE) was established by constitutional law. The concordat of 1933 between the Republic of Austria and the Vatican lay the ground for RE of the Roman Catholic Church. Only in 1946 a legislative act guaranteed RE as a school subject. Though RE is a compulsory subject, pupils can opt-out in the first ten days of the school year. When the required two-thirds majority for changes in educational legislation was rescinded the regulations for RE were specifically excluded.

RE is integrated in the curriculum as an 'ordinary' subject alongside others. However, it retains some particular features, of which the most important is the possibility for parents withdrawing their children and of students themselves opting-out once they reach the age of fourteen.

On the basis of a general separation of church and state, the state provides the space for the religious communities to offer religious education in school. The system is similar to the system in Germany (see Freudenberger-Lötz and Kraft in this volume); however the curricula are the exclusive responsibility of the religious communities and do not require state approval. The state's responsibility is to ensure that RE teaching is in accordance with the basic constitution. This means that RE in Austria adopts a confessional or denominational approach. Though the state controls the general frame of RE and pays the teachers, responsibility for its content and curricula lies with the churches and other religious communities. Uniquely in Europe, thirteen denominations and religious communities, including the Roman Catholic and various Protestant churches, are legally entitled to provide religious education in school.[1]

From the age of three children can attend kindergarten. These are supported by political parties, secular associations and the churches. Given the fact that 73.6% of the population is Roman Catholic, many kindergartens have a confessional orientation and approach RE in a distinctive manner. Though some care little about the subject, others begin the school day with prayer and others include Christian stories in the curriculum. Many kindergartens supported by political communities approach RE in a similar way.

---

1 These are the Roman-Catholic Church, The Evangelical Church (Augsburgian and Helvetican confession), the Greek Oriental (= Orthodox) church, the Greek Oriental congregation of the Holy Trinity, the Greek Oriental congregation of Saint George, Serbian-Greek Oriental congregation, Romanian Greek Oriental congregation, Russian Orthodox congregation, Bulgarian Orthodox congregation, Jewish community, Islam, Old Catholic Church of Austria, Evangelical Methodist Church, the Church of Jesus Christ of Latter-day Saints (Mormons) of Austria, Armenian-Apostolic Church of Austria, New Apostolic Church of Austria, Buddhist religious community of Austria, Syrian Orthodox Church of Austria, Coptic Orthodox Church of Austria.

There are, however, regional differences: unlike in Lower Austria, it is unusual for kindergartens in Vienna supported by political communities to provide RE.

This means that young children's knowledge of religion is different, and depends on the RE provided by parents and kindergartens. While some children start their primary education with some knowledge of Christian stories, many have no religious knowledge at all. However, since Austria is a Roman Catholic dominated country all children will have a basic knowledge of the great Christian festivals such as Christmas, Easter, and Epiphany, as well as other Roman Catholic festivals which are celebrated locally.

This chapter is written from the minority perspective of Protestant RE teachers in Austria, and shows how they try to teach those pupils who belong to their denomination.

Figure 1: The Austrian school system

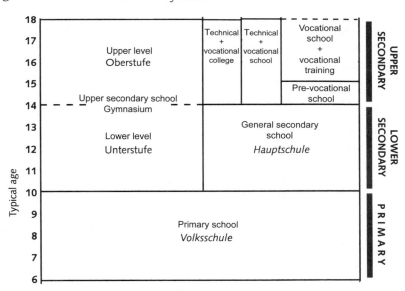

The organisation of Religious Education

As we have seen, Austria is a Roman Catholic dominated country. This means, for example, that in public primary schools teachers will often remember the saints (St. Nicolas, St. Barbara, St. Martin etc.). On the commemoration days of their respective patron saints schools will have holidays and – especially in the country – organise games or processions. Christmas, All Saints and Easter are included in the curriculum as a matter of course, without the necessity of special RE lessons. The celebration of First Communion normally takes place in Year Two. This is often treated as a festival for the whole year group, the theme is reflected in the curriculum and parents become involved. However this tradition is changing rapidly, especially in towns and districts where many Muslims and Orthodox children attend school. Whereas previously little consideration was given to the few Protestant children, this situation has now changed. Now inter-religious celebrations occasionally take place in schools that have a high percentage of non-Christian pupils. Another important issue in Year Two relates to the non-baptised children who usually attend the Roman Catholic or Protestant lessons: often these children are then baptised in the Catholic faith shortly before First Communion so that they can participate in these celebrations.

Religious services at the beginning and end of the school year and at Christmas and Easter are common in all public schools. According to the school and district, and depending on the number of religions practised there, these services are celebrated either as exclusively Roman Catholic, ecumenically or inter-religiously. Frequently these celebrations are supported by the class teacher and the school choir or orchestra.

Because of the Roman Catholic majority, only the Roman Catholic Church can teach RE across the whole country. Protestants are represented in many schools, but there are some areas where Protestantism is not present. At the same time, there are a few areas with a Protestant majority. For some time now Islam has played an increasing role in schools, mainly in the cities and larger towns.

Most churches and denominations are only able to provide RE in larger towns and cities, and some only in Vienna. A few churches delegate their RE provision: for example, Orthodox RE is delivered partly by the Roman Catholic church, and Methodist RE by other Protestant churches.

As a basic principle the child and the teacher have to belong to the same denomination. So a Roman Catholic child cannot take part in Protestant RE and vice versa. Only children who have no church affiliation are allowed to choose any form of RE.

In general Roman Catholic RE is taught two lessons a week, Protestant RE one lesson except in the Protestant areas, and Islamic RE one lesson. Only in some parts of Vienna, where a large number of Muslims live, there are two lessons a week.

The content of RE is the responsibility of the churches and for a long time decisions about content has been made without reference to other subject areas.

The curricula of Protestant RE has been based on the so called 'old Protestant system':
– Class One: Old Testament
– Class Two: New Testament
– Class Three: Church History
– Class Four: Theology and Ethics

In 1990 a general discussion started about school curricula, and in 1995 a new curriculum for the primary schools was introduced by the Ministry of Education. The Roman Catholic and Protestant churches took the opportunity to update their old curricula.

At the beginning of this process the traditional view, that the churches should develop their curricula independent from the state curricula, prevailed. Initially, the group that developed the Protestant RE curriculum paid little attention to the general state curriculum; however, new curriculum theory eventually influenced its thinking.

As a result, the group rejected the old content-based system that was focussed on cognitive teaching in favour of a more holistic approach. RE was no longer only about content and facts, but also about competencies – a key concept that became the main focus of the new curriculum.

A completely new situation came up when the Ministry of Education began to revise the curricula for secondary education. The traditional independence of the RE curricula was no longer in line with the new legal situation, and the churches had lost part of their autonomy. The Ministry of Education was surprised and a little distrustful about the attitude of the church: What do the churches want? What is their hidden agenda? However, as the churches took an active part in the debate, they accepted the general educational provisions and agreed that the religious aspects could be integrated.

The new curriculum is orientated towards aims. Autonomy is an important issue, and outcome competencies and learning methods a central focus. The teacher is seen as an integrated part of the process of learning.

Interestingly, the Muslim community in Austria started a similar process. This is a new challenge for our Austrian Muslim colleagues, as there is no comparable situation anywhere else in the world.

The confessional system of RE teaching in Austria does not only exist to protect minority interests. It is the important right of minority groups to have their own RE, given the fact that Austria does not have a multi-faith education system, but one organised around a dominant church and a variety of smaller denominations and religious communities. If there was only a single approach to the subject for all pupils, it would have the form of a general Roman Catholic RE.

It is now increasingly difficult to organise RE for both minority traditions and for the dominant Roman-Catholic church in the big cities. There you have a decreasing number of baptised children, and RE classes in Vienna are becoming smaller and smaller. This is why the Roman Catholic Church, the Protestant churches, and the Greek Orthodox Church are looking for new ways of cooperating in RE.

2. Methods and Example of Good Practice

Learning Methods in Primary Schools

The so-called 'open' or 'self-guided' learning is increasingly being used in Austrian primary schools. Several schools organise at least one class in an age group on the basis of alternative teaching methods and theory (e.g. Montessori, Peterson, Freinet). The main aim of 'self-guided' learning is that children learn to organise their work from the very beginning of their schooling. They receive weekly plans or sometimes a day's schedule of tasks they have to fulfil by the end of the stipulated period. This form of teaching is increasingly used in so-called 'integrated forms' in which children of different abilities are taught together. As the planned outcome is fixed by the teacher, it is possible for the children to achieve the aims and to experience a feeling of success. Additionally children learn to help each other and see that achievement and success can mean something different for each person and that not only the best, the quickest, and the loudest will gain the attention of the teacher. Morning group meetings or other forms of preparatory discussion are part of this form of teaching, as are excursions and meetings with experts either in the classroom or in their place of work.

Another important element of this method of learning is to teach pupils to use books and computers effectively. Many schools have a library or co-operate closely with the local library. Literature is no longer considered to belong exclusively to German lessons, but as part of general education and as a means of shedding light on pupils' lifeworlds.

Many primary schools – and in some cases even nursery schools – are equipped with computers and have internet access. Schools either have computer rooms or at least a few computers in classrooms. Whereas in the past children mainly used computers to access grammar learning programmes, exercises in mathematic, or games, they now use them to get information from the internet. Sometimes one of the planned tasks of the day or week can only be completed by using a computer.

Teaching Religious Education

What does this mean for religious education? As mentioned in the first part of the chapter, the number of pupils participating in RE varies enormously. Whereas in most schools in Austria the proportion of Roman Catholic pupils remains high enough to justify two lessons per week, the number of children belonging to other religious groups is normally less than ten, which means they only receive one lesson per week. In rural areas this can mean two lessons every fortnight.

This means that in Protestant RE children from different classes, and sometimes from different stages of education and even – in some regions – different schools come together for one lesson a week. The curriculum has to be flexible so that teaching can respond to the needs of all pupils. Though most children are used to work independently, they love listen to stories. Though it was common in the 1980s simply to tell a story and then to make a picture of it, nowadays teaching methods are more creative. Another difficulty is to organise the various age groups according to their different religious backgrounds. Children that take part in Protestant RE can come from a variety of backgrounds, including free evangelical churches and agnostic families, and many are not baptised. In addition, it is not always possible that the teaching takes place in the morning, because the pupils come from different classes. Some parents are not prepared to bring their children back to school in the afternoon, often because of work commitments, and the school timetable is planned in such a way that teaching in the afternoon is seen as a burden by both parents and children. This places the whole issue of RE in a negative context.

Learning at Various Stations: The Learning Circuit

Teaching and learning at different stations is a way to deal with all these difficulties. Each child can start where s/he feels comfortable, and while challenged to continue to work s/he can also step back to gather strength or express his/her views freely.

According to our experience children love to learn, but they also love to learn in a funny way. The use of learning stations can enable them to learn in ways that suit them best. If we are serious about respecting children and recognising their competences, and if we want them to be aware of this fact, then it is necessary to acknowledge their distinctive ways of learning. They learn alongside other pupils and need to accept the learning speed of their partner. For some children it is not always easy to find a partner for a station if one is required. In some groups there are disabled or younger pupils. The elder children may recognise that the pupil next to them has been given a much easier task than their own, and the reason for this must be explained so that nobody feels hurt or humiliated. The potential of group learning is enormous.

The basic idea is that children work independently, as far as possible, at different stations where appropriate learning material is available. It is important that the material and the tasks are prepared in such a way that the pupils can engage with it in their own individual style, taking account of the speed at which they work, the nature of the tasks, and the underlying pedagogy. As the stations are interconnected by both content and intellectual challenge, and are designed to be complementary, a comprehensive picture of a particular topic can be built up as pupils work their way through the learning circuit.

- *Standard stations*: As there is normally only one teacher available for RE lessons, for a range of pupils with different abilities and backgrounds, it is important that they can work independently at their stations. The level of independence can differ, depending on the extent to which the prepared material takes account of the background and context of the participating pupils. The nature of the set tasks must be clear and obvious for the pupils. They must know what they have to do to complete specific tasks. In some cases the materials will be challenging and may be responded to in different ways. Pupils should be able to assess their progress and develop self-control. A well prepared task will offer a variety of sources of information. However the material presented must not be too extensive and must be appropriate to each child's ability. It must be well structured with a clear introduction and explanation of the task.

- *External stations:* Theoretically, station work should activate as many senses as possible and utilise a wide range of learning methods. To achieve external sections are useful. They can be arranged in the corridor or placed in the library or can include outdoor tasks or be done at home (e.g. interviews).

- *Buffer stations:* In order to prevent the more able pupils to get bored so called 'buffer stations' may be set up. Here a number of extension tasks are offered. These might include: word puzzles, picture puzzles, and pictures to paint, i.e. tasks that will generate work that can be easily copied or reproduced.

- *Control and Service Station:* If possible the control of the work should result directly from the working material. This means that the correctness of the thinking process should originate from the produced object. It is not always possible however to provide so well prepared working material. For this reason a special control section is arranged where the pupils' working results can be compared with the correct answers.

- *Compulsory and Voluntary Sections:* Most learning circuits differentiate between basic learning material that all pupils should complete and extension material tailored to the interests of individual pupils. Hence there will be compulsory and voluntary stations, with a complete learning circuit consisting of an inner (compulsory) and an outer (voluntary) circle.

Impressions from the Learning Circuit

Issues of space must be taken into consideration: there is no sense planning to get children to make 'bricks' in the way the Israelites did in Egypt if there is no water in the room or if the floor covering is not suitable. If the room is particularly small it is normally possible to make use of the area outside the room. All pupils must have easy access to the stations. If it is not possible to arrange fixed stations, the material that is needed can be taken to each pupil's desk. For some stations a fixed position is needed, with enough space to work. This is always necessary, when experimental constructions or electricity and water access are needed, where the work at the sections requires space for movement, or where a high degree of noise is to be expected. A black board or a flip chart (wall map) can also be such a fixed section.

Which themes will be explored at the different stations? Basically any relevant aspect of the curriculum can be explored in this way: biblical themes, themes in church history such as the Reformation or the history of the local parish, world religions, the life and times of Jesus etc. The introduction or consolidation of a narrative cycle exploring the lives of a key religious figure (e.g. Abraham and Sarah, Joseph, Moses) is well suited to station learning and is popular among pupils.

Most teachers decide to work with sections if they are able to produce sufficient material and if they have sufficient time and space. Because many teachers have to work in different schools, it is not always possible to make the necessary preparation before the lesson.

We conclude with an example of a worksheet for the pupils to work through after hearing the story of Moses, Miriam, the Exodus and the Ten Commandments. This particular station was used to consolidate learning and for revision.

Moses, the Exodus and the Ten Commandments

My name:...

Date: ....

Compulsory Station

Tick the box when you have completed the station	x
Egypt (cooperative task). Choose a partner and complete the puzzle of the pyramide together. On a sheet of paper write down who the male members of the tribe have to get in touch with.	
The baby Moses (review of Moses childhood). Read the text and answer the questions on the sheet.	
10 plagues (initial task). Place the correct text under the pictures of the plagues.	

Exodus (cooperative task). Choose a partner and complete the domino run with sentences from the exodus story.	
The song of Miriam. Listen to the music using the headphones and read the words from the Bible.	
Ten commandments (crossword puzzle). Solve the puzzle based on the Ten Commandments.	
The golden calf (working sheet). Draw at least three people, using speech bubbles to show their words or thoughts.	
Devastation of Jericho. Look at the picture. How did the Israelites succeed in besieging the town. How did they do it? Write or draw this down on your sheet of paper. (Revision, written work).	

Voluntary stations

Food station: the Israelites fed themselves very simple during the 40 days of travelling. Try some of the food they would have eaten.	
The 12 families who left Egypt with Moses, Miriam and Aaron were called the 12 tribes. Solve the puzzle of the 12 tribal names.	
Sometimes the Hebrews felt as if they were lost in a labyrinth during their journey through the desert. Try the labyrinth worksheet to find a way through it.	

Perspectives

In Austria all pupils in primary schools receive RE lessons as a matter of course. It is a particular feature of RE in Austria that every child belonging to a registered religious community is entitled to at least one lesson per week in their own religion. With the increasing secularisation of the society, and an increasing number of not baptised children in primary schools, this state of affairs will certainly undergo a major change in the coming years. At present many of these children attend confessional RE because their parents had a religious upbringing and see it as the duty of the school to introduce their children to the basics of their religious tradition, such as the structure of the church year.

On the other hand, it is possible to recognise a trend towards the search for spiritual meaning. Parents are increasingly looking for ways in which they and their children can better cope with the challenges of life. This explains why many send their not baptised children to RE lessons. Nevertheless it is increasingly common for such pupils to change courses regularly. One year they might attend Roman Catholic RE, next year Protestant RE, and the following year they take no RE. This may have practical reasons, or due to personal choice. Such changes often happen without warning and can drastically reduce the number of children attending lessons. In addition, the birth-rate in Austria is decreasing and this influences the number of children in primary schools. As a result more and more smaller groups exist with children of different ages and abilities. The mix of ability means that it is important to use non-traditional teaching methods.

Our example of the station system is an ideal response to this situation. It is a method of teaching that has become increasingly popular in Protestant RE classes. Teachers meet to produce teaching material and exchange ideas about the practice of using stations to explore different themes in primary RE. Parents, who until recently considered this type of teaching as mere 'playing' now realise how much pupils learn and how motivated they can be.

In summary, we can conclude that RE will retain its place in primary schools in the near future. The subject's position was clearly defined in spring 2005 when the government changed the school laws but specifically excluded RE from these changes. The demands which these lessons place upon the teachers and their educational content are changing rapidly. The methodology of RE needs to be reconsidered and reoriented, including cooperation between subjects and the acceptance of assisted learning. Church congregations must also recognise that RE is no longer affiliated to their parish but has the status of an independent school subject. In some parts of Austria it is still usual that RE teachers work voluntarily in their parish, taking responsibility for children's welfare and development. The notion that the religious teacher is the connecting link between school, parents and parish will soon disappear and the church will have to take account of it.

References

Foidl, E., Martin, E., Miklas, H., Plank, M. & Schmall, Th. (2001) *Religionsunterricht – Oase im Schulalltag [Religious Education – An Oasis in daily school life]* (Wien, Evangelischer Presseverband).

Hilger, G., Leimgruber, St. & Ziebertz, H.-G. (2001) *Religionsdidaktik [Didactics of Religion]* (München, Kösel).

Frank, W. (Ed.) (2002) *Neue Lernkultur [New Culture of Learning]* Reihe Schulfach Religion, 21 (1+2) (Wien).

The Criteria for Good Religious Education Classroom Text Books in Bulgaria

Bojidar Andonov

1. Introduction

This chapter is concerned with the criteria for good religious education classroom text books in Bulgarian schools. The republic of Bulgaria is a parliamentary democracy. The population is made up of 7.71 million Bulgarians, 710,000 Turks, 313,000 Roma and a minority of 6,500 Armenians and Russians. The majority of the population is Christian (86%) and most of them belong to the Orthodox Church (82,6%). Islam is the second religion in numbers (12,2%).[1] After the political change in 1989 freedom of religion has been guaranteed.

2. Bulgarian School System, Primary Schools and Religious Education

We begin by looking back at the history of the Bulgarian school system. The first educational legislation in the principality of Bulgaria (1878) was based on the principles of democracy and decentralisation. After the founding of the Union of Bulgaria (1885) a more centralised school system was introduced with six years of compulsory education. When the communists came into power in 1944 the education system was closely linked to the establishment of the socialist system and the intention was that the education system should serve the socialist society. Though the school system in Bulgaria has not changed a lot since the collapse of communism in 1989, economy crises, demographic changes and developments in human and societal values have impacted upon it. Popov (2004) summarises the main positive conditions that have shaped the development of the education system after 1989: the abolition of socialist ideology and the influence of the communist party on the aims, administration and content of public education; respect for the freedom and initiative of the individual; initiatives to meet the educational needs of the pupils; diversification of curricula, with more freedom of choice for pupils concerning school courses, and the creation of opportunities for establishing private schools. The main responsibility for state education lies with the Ministry for Education, Science and Technology, while administration is shared on the regional, local and school level. An education reform

---

1 These facts are taken from the official site of the National Statistics Institute of Bulgaria. According to the US Democracy Commission (2006) the Orthodox Christians are 85% and Muslims represent 13% of the whole population of Bulgaria.

has taken place since 1990 with the adoption of four new education laws between 1991 and 2000.

The education system

Compulsory education in Bulgaria starts at the age of seven and ends at age 16. The school system includes 12/13 grades and is structured in the following levels:

a) Primary school
 – Class 1 to class 4 – elementary stage
 – Class 5 to 7/8 – pro gymnasium
b) Secondary school
 – Class 8/9 to 12/13
c) Higher education at universities, applied universities and colleges.

Primary education is provided in primary schools and the primary stages of basic schools. Private schools are few in number: Currently (2004) only eight private primary schools and 18 basic schools with a primary stage exist (Popov, 2004).

Figure 1: The Bulgarian school system

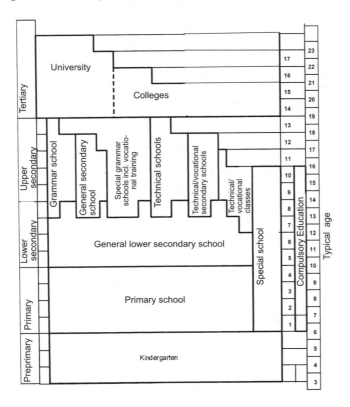

Under the new democratic government of Ivan Kostov (May 1997) initiatives were introduced to renew the debate about schooling and values. The following issues have been under discussion since that time: new roles for teachers, new teaching material and the re-introduction of religious education (RE). In the field of religious education the key task has been to take account of the new debates and to develop the teaching of RE along the lines of general educational criteria applied to all other subjects. This includes the principles for good textbooks, which is the main focus of this chapter. Before dealing with this specific issue, the general context of RE will be introduced.

Although resistance was expressed by socialist groups, the minister of education established a commission with the task to prepare for the introduction of RE in public schools. The commission was asked to work out a model for RE and also a teacher training programme. In the school year 1997/98 RE was introduced in grade 2 to grade 4 on a provisional basis. The main motivation for the re-introduction of RE was as follows: the decisive role of Christianity for the social, cultural and spiritual life of the people in Bulgaria; the new situation of religious freedom following a period of repression and stagnation; the re-awakening of the traditions and the cultural values of Christianity. RE in schools is seen as a central tool of the renewal of values in society.

Initiatives for teaching religion in schools

Religious education faced new obstacles with the election of a new socialist government in January 1995. However, in the autumn of 1997 the two main Bulgarian Theological Faculties (in Sofia and in Veliko Tarnovo), with the support of the Holy Synod, entered into a series of talks with officials from the Ministry of education officials that led to the formal introduction of RE in schools. It is important to understand how the Orthodox Church in Bulgaria reacted to the new approached to teaching religion in schools that followed from this decision. A summary of the internal debate within the Church will shed light on the current situation facing RE. The Holy Synod reacted only slowly and uncertainly to the new political situation in the country, and found itself criticised by both Bulgarian society as a whole and the Union of Priests. Since 1989 the Church hierarchy has failed to show confidence or long-term commitment to the new situation. Due to its internal difficulties, the Bulgarian Orthodox Church lapsed into a crisis that resulted in its split into two synods that lasted up to 1998.

On 30th September and 1st October 1998 in the St. Alexander Nevski Cathedral in Sofia an Orthodox Plenary Meeting was summoned to consult on the split in the Bulgarian Orthodox Church and seek ways to overcome its divisions. The heads of all Orthodox churches took part in a plenary meeting[2] that confirmed the Bulgarian Patriarch Maxim and the metropolitans as

2 See N.N. Resenija na Svetija razsiren sabor, Carkoven vestnik, No. 19/1-15.10.1998, 3.

the legitimate Holy Synod of the Bulgarian Orthodox Church. Though the six year split was surmounted *de jure, de facto* resentments still lingering on. Some representatives of the segregated 'Pimen-Synod' continue to convoke and refuse to return to the official Synod, under the conviction that Maxim is not the legitimate Patriarch of Bulgaria.

This description of developments within the Bulgarian Orthodox Church in recent years reveals the extent to which it has been concerned mainly with its own internal problems and is still reflecting on its role in the former communist system. Given that getting over the past is a precondition for approaching issues of the future, it is no surprise that the Church has been unable to offer the necessary support and commitment required for the task of vantage of developing the new concept of religious education in schools.

The re-introduction of RE in schools

The re-introduction of RE in public schools highlighted the central problem of the discord between the Church and the government and stimulated public discussion about the subject. The manifesto of the 'Union of Democratic Forces' for the mid-term elections included a commitment to the introduction of RE in public schools. When presenting the manifesto on 19th March 1997 Ass. Prof. Georgi Panev, the candidate of the 'Union of Democratic Forces' announced that '... the Union wants to introduce religious education in schools as an ordinary subject'.[3]

In April 1997, against the opposition of the socialists, Ivan Lalov, Minister of Education of the transitory government of Stefan Sofijanski and Rector of the Sofia University, convoked a commission to elaborate the project 'Religious education in the public schools'.[4] He mandated the commission, in pursuance with the relevant articles of the administrative legislation, to report to him by the 1st October on 'a project on the religious education in conformity with the methodical standards approved by the Ministry of Education'. [5] In a parallel move, on 28th August, the Ministry of Education sent a directive to the Head of the Regional Inspectorate of the Ministry of Education which stated: 'The Ministry of Education shall introduce in school year 1997/98 an experimental education in religion for children from the 2nd to the 4th grade. The education shall be performed in the schools by theologically instructed teachers as an optional subject.'[6] On the basis of the directive of the Ministry of Education, RE could be re-introduced in the state schools.

At first, RE was introduced only in grades 2, 3 and 4. In 1997 a series of text books 'Religija' (Religion) were published for grades 2 to 4; in October 1998 these were supplemented by volumes for the grades 5 to 6 and grades

---

3 Ivanova, A. (1997) SDS se gotvi da vavezda zadalzitelno veroucenie, in: *Duma*, 20.03.1997, 4.
4 Order of the Ministry of Education, Sciences and Technologies, No. RD 09-212/15.04.1997.
5 Order of the Ministry of Education, Sciences and Technologies, No.RD 09-336/20.05.1997.
6 Order of the Ministry of Education, Sciences and Technologies, No. 06-00-159/28.08.1997.

7 and 8. RE is now offered even in grade 1, for which a further text book has been produced. Grade 1 children are taught basic knowledge on religion, religious belief, divine service, the church, and ecclesiastical festivals. Wherever possible, pupils are given the opportunity to attend religious services during the school year. Before 2004/5 RE was referred to as a 'freely-selective-subject'; this meant that it stood alongside other optional schools subjects, and was not taught during the day within the normal school timetable. Since 2005/6, however, RE has been reclassified by the Ministry of Education as an 'obligatory-selective-subject' in state schools. There is no difference between 'freely' and 'obligatory' selective-subjects in terms of the school programme and the number of hours a week it is taught; rather, the difference lies in the remuneration of teachers and the nature of the organisation of the discipline during the school day.

According to information supplied by the Ministry of Education, in the school year 2006/7 religion was studied in 289 schools (an increase of 83 compared to the previous school year) by 16,600 children (an increase of 2,200). At present it is still not possible to offer religious education in all schools due to a lack of trained teachers.

Establishing a legal framework for RE

The re-introduction of RE came as no surprise to most observers; however neither Church nor the State were well prepared for it. As a result the subject regressed back to earlier practices that failed to take account of developments in teaching and learning in other subject areas. One of the reasons for this was the lack of a tradition of academic religious education in Bulgaria, a situation that continues to persist. The traditional catechetical approach has proved unsuitable for the intellectual complexities of open and critical discussion of religious issues in the classroom. This problem effects most areas of RE, and it can not be obviated easily and without problems. The establishment of a viable academic programme for the theory and practice of religious teaching raises many questions that, in my view, require urgent attention.

An important starting point for further reflection is the previously mentioned decree of the Ministry of Education in August 1997, through which RE was re-introduced in the Bulgarian public schools. In this decree the following grounds for introducing religious teaching were designated and set as objectives:
- cultural-historical reasons
- spiritual-moral reasons
- orientation towards the school traditions of Bulgaria
- orientation towards the Charter of the Human Rights
- orientation towards the Convention of UNO on the Children's Rights

- orientation towards the Constitution of the Republic of Bulgaria
- orientation towards the social and spiritual tendency of
  the Third Millennium.[7]

These principles offer a new and stable basis for religious education in Bulgaria, though they suffer from a lack of concrete detail. For example, the mention of cultural-historical reasons for studying religion raises the problem of the lack of interest and concern on the part of pupils. It is no longer self evident to them why they should obtain knowledge of, and reflect on, the historical role of the Bulgarian Orthodox Church, and of its Saints and martyrs during the period of Turkish domination and the period of communist persecution. They are more interested in answers to more basic and immediate questions related to their own lives. This suggests the need to ground RE in an anthropological approach: this would enable the subject to address questions immediately relevant to students in a more direct and convincing way than through the historical exploration of the Orthodox-Christian tradition; in addition, it could open up dialogue in the classroom with other Christian confessions and non-Christian religions.

What are the most urgent tasks of religious education in Bulgaria today?

Before the prohibition of religious instruction in 1947, the Orthodox Church used to define the contents of religious instruction. The questions and the answers based on the Orthodox Catechism were a constant factor; the only variable was the issue of teaching method and delivery of curriculum content to students. As a consequence of the re-introduction of religious teaching 1997 in the schools attempts are now being made in faculties of theology to establish religious education as an academic discipline. Even if the curriculum content remains constant, it should not be left to individual teachers to develop their own teaching methods. The issue of didactics is also an important one, especially given the history of religious education in Bulgaria. When didactics was primarily understood as a question of identifying curriculum content this discipline was of no importance for either the Catholic, Protestant, or Orthodox traditions because the content was already fixed. However, if didactics is understood within the new framework of general school education then other questions become significant: Why is an issue important for the students? What qualifications, skills and competences should students obtain for their lives now and in the future? This suggests that religious education, which has not traditionally been concerned with issues of curriculum content, now needs to commit itself to this discipline. There is a need to work toward persuasion, co-operation and debate in order to construct a significant religious pedagogy of this kind in Bulgaria.

---

7 See Andonov, 2000:358.

3. Good Textbooks as an Example of Good Practice in RE

For the convincing and successful implementation of religious education in Bulgarian schools, newly designed school books are urgently required. Hence a major task for religious pedagogy oriented towards the future is to collaborate conceptually and practically to develop new school books. The school books issued in 1997 and 1998 reflected a traditional understanding of the content and methods of religious education. This was largely due to the fact that church historians, Old and New Testament scholars, and Moral theologians wrote the text in the light of their understanding of their respective academic fields without any pedagogic concern for their organisation and arrangement. As a result they adopted a purely deductive understanding of didactics. A better understanding of didactics would see teaching religion as a process of delivering religious content in a way that relates it directly to the field of vision of the students, introducing them to ways of comprehend, implement and rearranging it. It is important that such didactical thinking is reflected in school text-books. This will require a widening of the focus of the curriculum to extend beyond a limited range of theological subjects to embrace a richer schematic content. First of all, the books have to be construed as forming a groundwork that gives teachers the option to embrace a variety of creative forms of teaching. This cannot happen unless the focus of the subject extends beyond that of the Bulgarian Orthodox tradition.

As an example, I present the text of a lesson from the textbook for grade two of the primary school. This will be followed by a commentary on the lesson. Because of the specific conditions in Bulgaria, no satisfactory textbook on the teaching of religion in schools has been produced so far. That is why I will dwell on an existing resource and, in commenting on its shortcomings, suggests ways in which better texts could be developed.

Example: Biblical Studies, Year 2

Lesson: The temptation of Jesus Christ in the desert (following Mt 4, 1-11; Lk 4:1-14; Mk 1:9-13)

Jesus Christ came on Earth to teach people to love God, love each other and help each other. But this was a very heavy task to comply with because people's sin incited them to do bad things. Jesus retreated into a desert. There He prayed unceasingly. Thus He prepared Himself to accomplish His work for the deliverance of the world. Filled with the Holy Spirit Jesus Christ spent 40 days and nights in the desert without eating or drinking anything. On the fortieth day He became hungry. Now the Devil appeared before Him to tempt Him.
'If You are the Son of God, tell these stones to turn into bread and You will satiate Yourself with them' – the Devil told Him.
Jesus Christ watched the stones. He could turn them into bread and satiate Himself. Yet this was not the aim of His deed. He wanted to give people spiritual food. That is why He answered:

'In the Holy Books it reads that man does not live by bread alone, but also by every Word that comes out of the Mouth of God.'

As he saw that in this way he would have no success, the Devil thought out another temptation. He brought Jesus to the Holy City of Jerusalem and went with Him up the roof of the Temple. There The Sly one told Him:

'If You are the Son of God, then throw Yourself down! In the Holy Books it reads that God will order His Holy Angels to carry You in their hands so that You do not bump Yourself to a stone.

Jesus could do this too, without being befallen by anything. And then, wouldn't everyone listen to His words? Yet God does not make use of such means. He does not want to convince us of His power through senseless deeds. People must come in a different way to the Faith in God and to the Love of God. They must understand how good and merciful He is and how big His Love for us is.

'Yes, but it reads also that you may not tempt The Lord, your God' answered Jesus. The Devil became embarrassed by these words, but he did not give his thought (intention) up. He led Jesus up a high mountain. From there he showed Him all the riches of the world with all their glory and spoke to Him:

'All the power and the splendour You see are mine. I can give them if I want to. I will give them to You if You fall down before me and supplicate me.'

But Jesus did not look for the power on the earth. His Kingdom is not a terrestrial one and is not material but spiritual and heavenly. Therefore He said to the Devil, 'Get away from Me, Satan! It reads that you shall worship only The Lord and serve only Him!'

As he saw himself powerless in the fight with Jesus Christ, the Devil left Him.

Everyone of us is subject to temptations. When we do believe in God and search for His Help we will defeat the temptations and Evil, and we will be successful in the good.

The retelling of the Gospel story is supplemented by the following text:

Unknown words:
Temptation – an enticing opportunity which becomes a sin for the one who takes it.

Questions:
a) Why did Jesus Christ come in this world?
b) How did Jesus Christ prepare Himself to accomplish His Work on earth?
c) Who tempted Jesus?
d) Explain why Jesus did not listen to the Devil.
e) To whom do we pray to defeat Evil?

A critical comment

This lesson forms part of a programme for pupils in the second grade of the primary school. The aim of the lesson is to learn that faith in God helps to defeat temptations and overcome evil. From an exegetic point of view the interpretation of this text is the same as that found in earlier religious text books. The text reduces the actions of Jesus to a moral level: he is presented as a teacher whose task is to direct people to live a morally good life. As a result pupils learn nothing about the deeper significance of the message of Jesus for life today: the announcement of the Kingdom of Heaven, which becomes a reality through his redemptive power. The teaching method employed in the text also relies on methods adopted in earlier school books: original biblical texts are supplemented with moral reflections without any concern to explore the theological meaning of the text and compare it with moral interpretations. A better approach would to start by presenting the biblical text itself, or retell it in a form closely linked to the original, and then explain the story by using different questions, examples and extended reflections in a manner that encourages debate in the classroom and addresses questions of the value of the text for pupils' lives today.

From the point of view of moral theology teachers could ask critical questions, such as whether the step from the faith in God to victory over evil is a simple one, thereby enabling pupils to reflect on how the story relates to their own lives. No explanation can be found in the lesson as to why Jesus Christ has to prepare Himself for his mission if He is actually God, why this preparation needed to take place in the desert, why it took forty days and nights, why He needed to fast. In addition, there is no explanation of Spiritual and Heavenly Kingdom. An interpretation of these and of similar issues would have made the lesson more theologically consistent and of greater value for the lives of pupils. The didactical structure of the teaching unit leaves no opportunity for extending and developing pupils' thinking. Instead the telling of the story and the posing of the questions constitute a one-dimensional block of meaning. No precise religious-didactical conception is recognizable here, because neither the textbook nor the curriculum includes any proposal for pedagogic elements that can penetrate into deeper and more complex levels of meaning.

As a result the educational objective of the lesson, the moral forming of the pupils, achieves no more than the theoretic transfer of knowledge. There is no attempt to address actual problems and queries in the pupils' horizons of experience, questions generated by a post-communist situation of cultural pluralism; and an absence of signs of correspondence between the actual lives of today's pupils and the content of the faith. The teachers are left to find a way forward by themselves, restricted by a teaching process that fails to orient the subject matter of religious education towards the lives of pupils.

4. Perspectives: Criteria for Teaching Material

Every text-book author is seeking to introduce their theological knowledge into the lessons they are drawing up in a manner that allows the children in the primary school to comprehend it. With regard to the construction of the teaching material, the present textbook shows no great difference from one from the 1940s. They follow the same structure:

(1) Introduction to the topic
(2) Presentation of the topic
(3) Repetition of the topic by means of questions.

The whole structure is oriented more towards a superficial understanding than to a deep comprehension of the meaning and its value for pupils' lives.

A modern alternative is to present the content in a way that is more tolerant towards matters of faith and nationality.

However, in general there is a lack of:

- a connection to the life-world of the pupils;
- ideas and proposals through which the pupils can be stimulated to a personal interpretation and explanation of the events;
- didactic concepts oriented towards the social and psychological needs and contexts of the pupils;
- a didactic enrichment of curriculum content designed to contribute to a better understanding of the subject;
- clearly defined aims for each instruction unit;
- methodological proposals for the orientation of the educational material in an appropriate way to the pupils' aptitudes;
- open ended learning rather than ex-cathedra instruction;
- teaching material which takes account of pupils' different abilities.

The text-book under review presents tasks that are purely cognitive in orientation and which favor those pupils who can understand texts at a glance and are linguistically capable of engaging in critical debate. There are few incentives for creative instruction and little orientation towards experience and action. Furthermore, alternative approaches to learning are absent: for example, through play primary school pupils can creatively express their thoughts in both verbal and non-verbal forms.

Most current textbooks are more or less extended school bibles with a form of presentation that prefers deductive ways of teaching. A modern school book should be more closely oriented towards inductive ways of teaching. A useful step forward would be to introduce a clearer differentiation of various sorts of texts: Biblical sources, legends, explanations, proverbs, materials for a further study, etc. Moreover, a textbook designed for pupils could give further stimuli for different forms of learning (individual work, work in partnership, in groups, project works etc.) and present factual material not only verbally, but also graphically, in the form of drawings, pictures, comics, etc.

References

Andonov, B. (2000) *Der Religionsunterricht in Bulgarien. Geschichte, Gegenwart und Zukunft religiöser Bildung in der orthodoxen Kirche Bulgariens [Religious Education in Bulgaria. History, Present and Future of Religious Education in the Orthodox Church of Bulgaria]* (Essen, Die Blaue Eule).

Popov, N. (2004) Bulgarien, in: H. Döbert, W. Hörner, B. von Kopp & W. Mitter (Eds.) *Die Schulsysteme Europas [The Education Systems in Europe]* (Hohengehren, Schneider), 61-74.

Appendix 1

Religion textbook for 1st grade of the Bulgarian state schools

Religia za 1 klass	Religion for he 1st grade
ОСНОВНИ ТЕМИ	**Main themes**
I. Аз съм християнче – 5 часа	**I. I am a Christian – 5 lessons**
1. Иисус Христос – Син Божий	1. Jesus Christ – Son of God
2. Света Дева Мария – Божията Майка	2. Saint Virgin Maria – the Mother of God
3. Храмът – дом Божий	3. The church building – God's home
4. Молитвата – разговор с Бога	4. The prayer – a talk with God
5. Как да се държим в храма	5. How to behave in the church
II. Нашите християнски празници – 2 часа	**II. Our Christian feasts – 2 lessons**
1. Светците – Божии хора	1. The saints – people of God
2. Моят светец – моят имен ден	2. The name of my saint guardian and the feast day of my name
Ш. Вярата в Бога ни прави добри и силни – 2 часа	**III. Faith in God makes us better and stronger – 2 lessons**
1. Света Петка – Петковден	1. St Petka – the day/the feast of St Petka
2. Свети Димитър – Димитровден	2. St Dimitar – the day/the feast of St Dimitar
IV. Ангелите - наши пазители – 1 час	**IV. The Angels – guardians of the Christians – 1 lesson**
1.Свети Архангел Михаил – Архангеловден	1. St Archangel Michail – the day/the feast of St Archangel Michail
V. Бог подкрепя праведните и прави чудеса – 2 часа	**V. God helps the righteousness and performs miracles – 2 lessons**
1. Свети Николай Чудотоворец – Никулден	1. St Nicholas the Miracle-Performer – the day/the feast of St Nicholas
2. Свети Игнатий Богоносец – Игнажден	2. St Ignatius the God-Bearer – the day/the feast of St Ignatius
VI. Рождество Христово – 2 часа	**VI. Christmas – 2 lessons**
1. Витлеемската звезда	1. The star of Betlehem
2. Коледа	2. Koleda (Christmas Eve)

VII. Кръщението на Иисус Христос – 2 часа	**VII. Jesus Christ's Baptism – 2 lessons**
1. Богоявление – Йордановден	1. Epiphany – the day/ the feast of Epiphany
2. Свети Йоан Кръстител – Ивановден	2. St John the Baptist – the day/ the feast of St John the Baptist
VIII. Да обичаме всички хора – 1 час 1. Прошка	**VIII. We should love all people – 1 lesson** 1. Forgiveness
IX. Света Дева Мария – благословена от Бога – 2 часа	**IX. Saint Virgin Maria – blessed by God – 2 lessons**
1. Благата вест – Благовещение	1. The Blessed Annunciation – the day/ the feast of the Annunciation
X. Славим името на Иисус Христос – 2 часа	**X. Let's glorify Jesus Christ's name – 2 lessons**
1. Влизане на Иисус Христос в Йерусалим – Цветница	1. The entry of Jesus Christ in Jerusalem
2. Христос възкресе – Великден	2. Christ's Resurrection – the day/ the feast of Easter
XI. Доброто побеждава злото – 1 час	**XI. The good is victorious over the evil – 1 lesson**
1. Свети Георги Победоносец – Гергьовден	1. St George the Victorious – the day/ the feast of St George
XII. Светите братя Кирил и Методий – 2 часа	**XII. The saints Cyril and Methodius – 2 lessons**
1. Животът на светите Братя	1. The life of the saint Brothers
2. Подготовка за празника на славянската писменост	2. Preparation for the feast of the Slavic alphabet and literature
общо: 25 часа	**Totalling: 25 lessons (a school year)**

Pupil-to-Pupil Dialogue in Religious Education in England and Wales

Derek Bastide

Introduction

The example of good primary practice in England and Wales focuses on pupil dialogue. We begin by giving an overview of the organisation of religious education, focusing especially on the 1988 Education Reform Act, the development of local agreed syllabuses and the establishment of attainment targets. We then describe the work of Julia Ipgrave, whose empirical research into children's conversations about religion has led to the development of 'Dialogical RE' – an approach to teaching and learning that seeks to enrich pupils' understanding of religion by stimulating classroom discussion.

1. The Organisation of Religious Education

It was in 1870 that the Government legislated for the compulsory schooling of all children in England. Prior to this many children were being educated in schools provided overwhelmingly by the churches, Anglican, Protestant and latterly Roman Catholic. These schools continued, but in areas where there was a shortage of school place the Government 'filled the gaps' by building new schools, known as Board schools as they were the responsibility of the recently created School Boards. In this way the dual system of education came into being in which voluntary schools (almost exclusively church schools) and community schools (as the Board schools are now called) exist side by side. Religion in the voluntary schools was according to the school's denomination; in the new board schools it should not be 'by means of any catechism or formulary which is distinctive of any particular religious denomination'.

The twentieth century saw many developments in the dual system. Without going into details there are two types of voluntary schools, 'aided' and 'controlled'. The former is entitled to provide both collective worship and religious education according to its own denomination's teaching while the latter provides collective worship according to its trust deeds but the RE it provides is drawn from the same agreed syllabus as that in place for community schools. The vast majority of voluntary schools are either Anglican or Roman Catholic. There is a small number of Jewish schools and very recently the first Muslim and Sikh voluntary aided schools have been established. Known for generations as 'church schools' there is now a tendency to refer to them as 'faith schools'. They are currently enjoying considerable popularity with parents.

One of the great challenges for the education system in the latter part of the twentieth century has been the increasing presence of children from ethnic minorities on school rolls. The general approach adopted has been one of *multiculturalism* with its emphasis upon integration rather than assimilation. RE is seen as an important contributor to this process and has adapted itself over the years not only by teaching about the major faiths in the country but also by fostering empathy and understanding among pupils and communities so that all should respect both their own way and the ways of others.

The example of good practice chosen sits very firmly with those two main focuses of pupils learning about the religions in a sensitive and empathetic way and through this of themselves becoming both more aware of their own faith for life. Julia Ipgrave (Ipgrave, 2001) has developed a process she calls Dialogical RE in which she places pupils, properly prepared, in dialogue settings in which she herself acts as a facilitator. This dialogue setting gives pupils both the opportunity to engage with fellow pupils usually but not always of different religious traditions face to face and to share different beliefs and values in order both to learn more first hand more about other traditions and also to develop the beliefs and values they themselves hold.

This work is discussed later in the chapter and it will be argued that Dialogical RE has a particularly powerful potential role is developing the key aims of RE.

Primary Education

Formal education in England is compulsory from the ages of 5 to 16 years and for the majority of children and young people this takes place in school, although there are a few children who are educated at home. The Education Reform Act, 1988 designated four *key stages* within these compulsory years: Key Stage 1 (5 to 7 years), Key Stage 2 (7 to 11 years), Key Stage 3 (11 to 14 years) and Key Stage 4 (14 to 16 years). Year groups range from Year 1 (5 to 6 years) to Year 11 (15 to 16 years).

Of these, children in Key Stages 1 and 2 are classified as primary age children. However there is an important modification to this. Children enter Key Stage 1 at the beginning of the school term after their fifth birthday. However virtually all children enter school at the beginning of the school year in which they will become five, many initially on a half time basis. These children are placed in the *Reception class* and they have a special curriculum based on six themes rather than the subjects of the National Curriculum which they will begin when they enter Key Stage 1. Therefore most primary schools have an age span of 4 to 11 years. Although many primary schools have the full primary age range, in many towns there will be *infant schools* which cater for Foundation and Key Stage 1 pupils and *junior schools* who have pupils from

Years 3 to 6. There are in a small number of areas in England, schools arranged as First and Middle schools taking pupils from 4 to 12 years but these are tending to be reorganised into 4 to 11 schools as this fits in better with the key stage structure.

Figure 1: The school system in England and Wales

Age	Key Stage	Year	School
Post-compulsory education/upper secondary and post secondary level:			
16-18+			Further education: Sixth form college Further education college Tertiary college
16-18+			Secondary school
Compulsory education:			
15-16	Key Stage 4	11	Secondary Education: All-through comprehensive school, comprehensive school, city technology college, secondary modern school
14-15		10	
13-14	Key Stage 3	9	
12-13		8	
11-12		7	
10-11	Key Stage 2	6	Primary Education
9-10		5	
8-9		4	
7-8		3	
6-7	Key Stage 1	2	
5-6		1	
4-5	Foundation Stage		Reception class in primary school

The Education Reform Act 1988

The Education Reform Act of 1988 brought dramatic changes to the education system of England. It introduced a National Curriculum, assessment (with school league tables based on results) and a robust programme of inspection and reporting. The aim of all these changes was to produce a common curriculum to which all pupils are entitled. The aim of this 'balanced and broadly based curriculum' is to promote 'the spiritual, moral, cultural, mental and physical development of pupils at the school and of society' (ERA, 1988:section 1:2). The National Curriculum consisted of English, mathematics, science, technology, history, geography, music, art, physical education and, in secondary schools, also a modern foreign language. Each of these subjects, called foundation subjects, had prescribed national attainment targets and programmes of study. The original intention was that all these subjects should be assessed in national tests but this proved to be unrealistic so the assessment was limited to only three subjects, English, mathematics and science, which were regarded as *core* subjects. Over the years there have been adjustments to the requirements of the National Curriculum to make it more workable and to be sufficiently flexible to respond to individual needs.

The 1988 Education Reform Act had a revolutionary effect on both schooling and teaching. It reduced the level of teacher autonomy and teacher freedom especially in primary schools. Now that the National Curriculum subjects were compulsory with the content in a broad sense laid down and backed up by inspection and reporting, teachers were no longer in a position, if they wished, to neglect subjects in which they were less confident: they all had to be done! For RE, which had often been a subject squeezed out if the week was proving to be particularly busy, this was a very welcome development.

Teachers in primary schools are expected to teach across the whole curriculum and students training to teach children in the Foundation stage, Key Stage 1 and Key Stage 2 have to provide evidence of this broad competence in order to gain qualified teacher status. Sometimes music is taught across a school by a specialist on the staff and in some schools there is an element of semi specialist teaching in English and mathematics in Years 5 and 6 but apart from that the class teacher takes responsibility for the whole curriculum. Normally therefore all class teachers are responsible for teaching RE to their classes. Few teachers have expertise across every subject in the curriculum so schools have to develop a system which enables teachers to teach the range of subjects knowledgeably and effectively. The way that schools tend to tackle this issue is through *subject coordinators or subject leaders.*

The way this works is that each teacher (except normally for teachers in their first year of teaching) is given the responsibility of coordinating and leading a subject. In a small school teachers may have this responsibility for more than one subject. The role of the RE co-ordinator (and co-ordinators for all subjects will have essentially the same role) includes taking a lead role in the planning of the subject across the school, selecting and acquiring resources such as books, artefacts and DVDs to support the teaching, providing support, advice and (where necessary) subject knowledge to colleagues, monitoring the teaching of RE in the school and co-ordinating assessment and record keeping. Such a system inevitably works unevenly across primary schools: one school may have an RE co-ordinator with a specialist qualification in the subject while another may have an RE coordinator drafted because there happened to be a vacancy upon appointment to a teaching post in the school. However evidence suggests that the system works reasonably well and teachers grow into their subject (Bastide, 1999:chapter 2).

The Place of Religious Education

So where does RE stand in all of this? (Bastide, 1992, 1998, 2006). Clearly it isn't in the National Curriculum but it is compulsory. The Education Reform Act (ERA, 1988) talks of a Basic Curriculum which consists of the National Curriculum and religious education (RE). This ensures that RE is equal in status and standing with the subjects of the National Curriculum but not subject to the nationally prescribed Attainment Targets, Programmes of Study and assessment arrangements which are required of them. But if the content of RE is not laid down nationally who decides what that content should be? The Act established three key features:

- A *broad framework* to guide the content of RE
- Local control of the content of RE through an *agreed syllabus*
- A watch dog in each local education authority to oversee arrangements, *the Standing Advisory Council for Religious Education (SACRE)*.

The *framework* in which future RE should be set is very brief – one sentence only – but highly significant. The 1988 Act laid down that all new agreed syllabuses must:

> reflect the fact that the religious traditions in Great Britain are in the main Christian whilst taking account of the teaching and practices of the other principal religions represented in Great Britain.

Here for the first time the law lays down a requirement about the content of RE. For example, an agreed syllabus which includes only Christianity would not be within the law and also neither would one which attempts to exclude it.

Key Issues

In unpacking this brief framework, a number of issues emerge some of which raise questions which are not actually resolved in the Act.

- It is important to note that the framework refers to religious traditions (in the plural) and while Christianity is acknowledged as the main one it is also seen as one of a number of religious traditions within the country. The religious composition of Great Britain is therefore seen as pluralist. This has implications for RE in community schools. While it is not stated explicitly, there is the implicit assumption that RE is more concerned with developing awareness and understanding of religion and of religions than it is with any confessionalist or nurturing intent.
- The Act is very clear about the criteria for the selection of the religions to be included in the agreed syllabuses: in addition to Christianity, they

should be the other principal religions represented within Great Britain. This geographical context is extremely important and has implications in three directions. Firstly the religions to be studied are those which children will come across in moving around Great Britain. Therefore schools are not licensed to teach little known religions from remoter parts of the world but those which are significant in this country. Secondly it means that local educational authorities in which the presence of other religious traditions is not numerically significant must still base their agreed syllabus upon the religious composition of Great Britain. Thirdly it implies that RE should be an agent to help pupils to understand the beliefs, values and practices of their fellow citizens in a multicultural society and so paves the way for the development of social inclusion as major aim of RE.

– Although the Act as we have seen requires that the other principal religions in Great Britain should appear in all new agreed syllabuses nowhere does it indicate which religious traditions these should be. Despite early fears that this might be an area of high controversy, Buddhism, Hinduism, Islam, Judaism and Sikhism seem to have been widely accepted. Certainly these are the ones which figure strongly in agreed syllabuses around the country.

– Nowhere does the Act give guidance on the balance to be given to the different religious traditions within syllabuses apart from the general implication that Christianity, because of its position as the main religious tradition, should have the most time. Here it is interesting to note that this was solved effectively by the Model Syllabuses (1994), non-statutory guidance from the Schools Curriculum and Assessment Authority (SCAA) to Local Education Authorities, which worked on the basis that Christianity should receive 50% of the RE curriculum time. Although these Model Syllabuses were purely advisory and without any legal standing, they have proved to be highly influential. The near universal practice now is for Christianity to have half the available time.

– The Act lays down no requirements about which religions should be taught at which points over a school career and there were fears that six year old children, say, might have to study six religions over the school year: this would be very confusing for the children and do little justice to the religions themselves. Again the Model Syllabuses came to the rescue with their guidance that children in Key Stage 1 should study Christianity and one other religion and in Key Stage 2 should study Christianity and two other religions. A number of agreed syllabuses have, for example, laid down that in Key Stage 1 it should be Christianity and Judaism and in Key Stage 2, Christianity, Hinduism and Islam.

Local Provision

At a time when education was coming increasingly under national control, the local nature of RE was being reaffirmed. The act required that each local education authority should produce its own agreed syllabus for Religious Education within its own jurisdiction or, failing that, adopt the agreed syllabus of another local education authority. Many suggestions have been made as to why RE was not made a National Curriculum subject: church schools had their own church based syllabuses which would differ, the right of withdrawal was still there, it was feared that agreeing a national syllabus might prove controversial and divisive. Whatever the reason RE remained firmly in local hands. The agreed syllabus was so called because it should be agreed by those groups which were presumed to have an interest in the RE taught in the local schools: these were the general public (through their elected councillors), teachers, the Church of England and lastly other Christian traditions and other faiths in the local community. This grouping formed a Standing Conference which recommended the agreed syllabus to the Local Education Authority for approval. The final approval comes from the Secretary of State for Education and Skills. Once accepted this would provide the basis upon which a school would draw up its scheme of work. There was considerable freedom in drawing up the agreed syllabus but all must conform to the framework discussed above. One agreed syllabus, for example, laid down Christianity and Judaism for Key Stage 1 pupils as Judaism was a significant faith in the area and so would provide first hand experience for young children through activities such as visits to synagogues and therefore be more accessible to them. Another agreed syllabus from a local education authority in another part of the country chose Christianity and Sikhism for the same reason.

Over the years since 1988, concerns have been raised about this local development of agreed syllabuses. A study of agreed syllabuses indicates that they vary considerably in quality and, in the drive for the continual improvement of educational standards in English schools, this variation has made the task much harder for RE. There have been attempts to encourage greater uniformity. The Model Syllabuses (SCAA, 1994) referred to earlier, the Exemplification of Standards Key Stage 1 and 2 (Qualifications and Curriculum Authority, 1998) which teachers embraced with enthusiasm and which cut across all agreed syllabuses, Non-Statutory Guidance on RE (QCA, 2000) and finally the high profile non-statutory National Framework for RE (QCA, 2004) which will be discussed later. All these initiatives are non-statutory and therefore could be completely ignored by those developing agreed syllabuses but slowly they are bringing RE syllabuses across the country closer together.

Religious Education in the local area is overseen by a *Standing Advisory Council for Religious Education (SACRE)*. Its chief function as laid down in the Education Reform Act is to:

> advise the authority upon such matters connected with religious worship in county schools and the religious education to be given in accordance with an agreed syllabus as the authority may refer to the council or as the council may see fit (ERA, 1988:11.1a).

Matters dealt with are likely to focus upon such matters as teaching methods, the choice of teaching materials, the provision of in-service training for teachers, curriculum guidance arising from the agreed syllabus and the monitoring of school inspection reports with special reference to RE. Much of the work is advisory but there is one very specific responsibility with reference to RE: to require the Local Education Authority to review its agreed syllabus.

The membership of a SACRE is based on the same four groupings as make up the Agreed Syllabus Conference though the individual members may be different.

Attainment Targets

Although we have noted the localism of agreed syllabi there is very broad and general agreement across the country, supported too by government initiatives that a full programme of RE must include both a knowledge and understanding of religions and the encouragement of pupils to be reflective in applying what they are learning to their own personal search for meaning. In most agreed syllabuses there are two parallel and interconnected attainment targets: learning *about* religion and learning *from* religion. Different agreed syllabuses may use different words but essentially these two phrases encompass them all. It is the two attainment targets together which constitute good RE.

Learning *about* religion as the term suggests, is learning about religions, their beliefs and practices and so on. However it is important that this should be done in a way which links understanding and empathy with factual knowledge. It means encouraging pupils to ask both 'how' and 'why' questions. It is quite possible to teach a unit of work on the Hajj, to make a diary of the happenings on each of the days of the pilgrimage and to describe these with great enthusiasm and still to leave the pupils with no awareness of the significance of pilgrimage and why Muslims will save up all their lives to undertake it. Similarly it is possible to teach a factual topic on fasting drawing the material from a range of religious traditions and still leave the pupils thinking that this is a very odd and eccentric way to behave! Both these would count as bad practice. Teaching about religions insensitively can lead to negative attitudes, prejudice and stereotyping which runs exactly counter to a major purpose of RE in schools.

Learning *from* religion is the other focus of RE and it is concerned to help pupils to reflect upon what they are learning about religions and to begin to relate it to their developing view of the world. This relates very closely to spiritual development to which RE is a major contributor in the school. It is very important that pupils are helped to see that religions deal with matters which are fundamental to humanity, questions of purpose and value, and to begin to ask these questions of themselves to help them in their own personal search. These will include 'ultimate questions' such as 'why are we here?' 'is there a purpose?' 'why be good?'. Learning from religion can come in less dramatic form. A group of Y5 pupils (9-10 years) were doing work on the Feast of Pesach and during this they looked at the background setting, the structure of the meal and the practical symbolism of the different objects on the seder plate. In discussions, which arose within the lessons, pupils raised a number of issues: the importance of freedom, the importance of remembering and celebrating significant events in a community or group, the value of belonging to a group and how a shared experience could hold together a community of people over thousands of years. This is a summary of the discussion – not the actual words used – but it indicates a growing reflectiveness in the pupils which can enrich their own search.

It is fair to say that many class teachers in primary schools who are not RE specialists tend to be more at ease with the first attainment target and find the second attainment target much more daunting than the first. Almost certainly it is largely a question of confidence which will develop over time. It is one of the challenges that the RE co-ordinator in the primary school has to try to meet.

National Framework for Religious Education (QCA, 2004)

It has been noted already that the local control of RE can be both a strength and a weakness. That it allows local education authorities to reflect the special conditions of their area in their agreed syllabus is a strength but the considerable variation in quality between different syllabus is a weakness in an education system which is focusing strongly upon the raising of standards across the board. Because of the increasing popularity of RE as a public examination subject in secondary schools and also because of the potentially important role that RE can play in developing understanding in a multiracial and multifaith society, the Secretary of State for Education and Skills requested the Qualifications and Curriculum Authority to develop a framework for RE which, although non-statutory, would be a powerful guide and steer to Agreed Syllabus Conferences when reviewing their agreed syllabus, a task which has to be undertaken every five years. The framework under-

went extensive consultation with interested parties and received very positive and widespread backing. Essentially the framework provides detailed
guidance on how RE can be taught so that pupils not only learn about religion but can learn from it too. It sets out ways in which pupils can develop
their knowledge, understanding and skills and suggests levels of attainment
that they should achieve.

In the launch of the National Framework on October 28th 2004, two powerful contributions which RE could make to the curriculum were noted:

– Religious education can transform pupils' assessment of themselves and
  others and their understanding of the wider world. It is vital in widening
  inclusion, understanding diversity and promoting tolerance.
– Religious education has a vital role to play in providing pupils with a
  range of experiences that enable them to develop a realistic and positive
  sense of their own beliefs and ideas.

Here we have confirmed and included all the developments which have been
noted over the years. In these quotations we have the two attainment targets
with a special focus for each: for social inclusion and for spiritual development. Good practice in RE in England very simply reflects all these.

2. Methods and Example of Good Practice

There are naturally very many examples of good practice around but a recent
one which has captured the imagination and interest of many RE specialists
in the country is the development work of Julia Ipgrave, namely her two
projects: Pupil-to-pupil dialogue in the classroom as tool for religious education (Ipgrave, 2001) and Building e-bridges (Inter-faith dialogue by email)
(Ipgrave, 2003). Both projects are closely related and though their contexts are
different they have similar aims. The work on the first project is class based
with pupils engaged in dialogue face to face with others in their class in their
primary school in Leicester. The work of the second, essentially an extension
of the first, involves dialogue by email communication between pupils in
different schools, either local or in more far flung counties such as Cumbria
in the far north and East Sussex in the deep south but importantly schools
which have pupils of a different religious background. It is, of course, not always necessary to have dialogue groups composed of pupils from different
religious traditions as each individual tradition is by no means uniform. The
first project (Ipgrave, 2001) will be the one considered here.

Ipgrave calls her work *Dialogical RE* but it is not a new form of RE but an
enriching approach which draws upon existing RE and develops it, changing
what can so often be an inert content based, albeit interesting, subject to one
which is active and alive. It is more a process which draws on subject content
than being subject content itself. Regular RE will still continue: pupils will

still make visits to places of worship, will still explore the use of artefacts, will still undertake topics on Sacred Books, the Life of Jesus and Pesach and the like, will have visiting speakers from faith traditions and so on. Dialogue is, of course, not new to the primary school – it is often used in the English curriculum – but is new to primary RE, at least in the form that Ipgrave uses it, perhaps because many teachers feel less confident in the subject area and because exploring religious beliefs can be seen by some as a sensitive area and so best avoided.

In Pupil-to-Pupil Dialogue, Ipgrave established dialogue groups in classrooms in the primary school in which she taught in Leicester, an industrial town in the English East Midlands with a strong presence of ethnic minority groups in its population; in her school 85% of the pupils come from Muslim families. The occasional paper (Ipgrave, 2001) details to some extent her research but is particularly concerned to discuss the implications of this work which she has pioneered for encouraging and promoting dialogue between primary school children on a much wider scale.

In the paper, Ipgrave gives two examples of Dialogical RE which she has established in her school. In the first three Year 6 pupils (one Hindu girl, one Rastafarian boy and one Christian girl) along with Ipgrave as the teacher/ facilitator are devising questions and issues to be used by other pupils in their dialogue sessions. In the second a group of Year 4 pupils (one Hindu boy and two Christian boys) along with Ipgrave is responding to one of the questions prepared by the Year 6 group, 'How many gods do you think there are?'.

Naturally the key term in Ipgrave's work is dialogue so it is essential to understand what she means by dialogue and what is involved in engaging in the activity. She identifies a threefold developing understanding of dialogue, primary, secondary and tertiary, ranging from the acknowledgement of different experiences, viewpoints and influences on pupils' behaviour (primary dialogue) to promoting an atmosphere in the classroom in which pupils are happy to share their views with others, to listen to others with respect and are prepared to make changes in their perspective on the world and on religion (secondary dialogue) and finally to establish learning activities in the classroom which enable dialogue to take place (tertiary dialogue).

It is clear from this that dialogical RE draws upon pupils' existing understanding of religions built from home, friends, the media, RE lessons and so. By placing pupils in these dialogue settings it brings them up closely to different religious traditions and encourages them to *think* about these experiences and to build them into a coherent framework. Dialogue settings provide the necessary opportunities for pupils to talk thoughtfully and respectfully with each other so as to understand the religious viewpoints of others, to reflect upon their own beliefs and attitudes and provides the opportunity for adjustments and developments to be made. This is quite a different activity from the sort of discussion based on ignorance which can so easily occur in RE lessons or the unthinking presentation of opposing views.

'To understand what Dialogical RE is it is also important to recognise what it is not. Firstly it is not another term for any form of verbal interchange in the RE lesson. The elements of collaboration and search for meaning need to be present. Dialogical RE is not just an exchange of differing points of view ('alternating monologues'), but requires an interplay between them; does child A agree with what child B has said; does child C develop any of her ideas in the light of what she has heard from child D; or is it possible to draw child E and child F's thoughts together?' (Ipgrave, 2001:20).

Clearly the great challenge for Dialogical RE is establishing the right atmosphere and relationship in a class which will enable this openness and sharing to take place. For this to happen there need to be trust in the dialogue groups so that pupils feel able to make their contributions. There needs to be a willingness to accept that each individual's contribution is of importance and that all in the group must be included in the activity. Ipgrave recognises that many teachers, if they want to develop Dialogical RE in their classes and schools, will need to do preparatory work and she offers both very helpful advice and useful strategies (Ipgrave, 2001:22-27).

Why is it good practice?

Good practice is itself an interesting term. For the purposes here it is assumed that for any teaching to be 'good practice' it must meet both general educational and subject specific criteria. This means at least that the material taught must be clear, well planned and appropriate to the age and stage of the pupils. Very importantly too the subject material must be accurate. Pupils should have a degree of active engagement in their learning and it is very helpful too if the learning can be enjoyable. In subject terms for RE teaching to be 'good practice' it should fit within the aims and purposes of RE which have been developing over a number of years and found more recent expression in the twin attainment targets the publications of the Qualifications and Curriculum Authority and of the very recent National Framework.

There are many strengths in Dialogical RE which makes it an example of good – many would say excellent – practice. These strengths are naturally in RE but they also overflow into other very important aspects of the broad curriculum.

If we take RE itself, the two overriding attainment targets – learning about religion and learning from religion are both met very strongly by Dialogical RE. In dialogue pupils learn at first hand what pupils of other faiths believe and practice but in an active way: there is discussion, there is questioning, there is challenge. From listening and comparing they learn that there is di-

versity within religious traditions – unlike the primary school text books
which present religious traditions as so clear cut and monochrome. Engaging
in this activity they also are able to learn so much from religions as the process requires them to think, to reflect upon what they believe and value, to
evaluate it and perhaps to make adjustments in their own understanding as
a result of the process. An engagement in this dialogue, providing that it is
thoughtful and self confident, can be a very powerful aid in developing and
refining their own search for meaning.

The National Framework for Religious Education (QCA, 2004) emphasised two major focuses for RE in the school closely related to the two attainment targets discussed above: social inclusion and spiritual development.
Through Dialogical RE pupils are put in the position of having to engage
face to face with other pupils many of whom who bring to the school values, beliefs and practices which are different from their own. The process requires them to have a willingness to listen and not to condemn out of hand.
It should also engender a deepened sensitivity to the feelings and ideas of
others and a willingness to learn, to respect other views and so to extend the
limits of their tolerance. In the longer term it could encourage pupils to value
differences and to become open minded people. Regular RE teaching in the
classroom can meet a number of these issues; Dialogical RE builds upon that
work to bring the pupils' understanding into a much stronger focus.

Dialogical RE fosters spiritual development in very similar ways. The role
of the dialogue in providing pupils with the opportunity to hear alterna-
tives and through this to reflect upon what they already have in the way of
beliefs, values and attitudes is a central plank of spiritual development. In
dialogue 'ultimate' questions will inevitably arise which, in turn, provide a
hard focus for thought and reflection. If properly handled the process of dialogue should lead to a refining and clarifying (but not necessarily changing
fundamentally) an individual's beliefs and encourage a growing confidence
in expressing them.

Looking at more general skills and attitudes which are central to the curriculum as a whole, three areas to which Dialogical RE can contribute particularly strongly are
- *Thinking*. At the heart of successful dialogue is thinking. Pupils in dialogue hear views which sound strange and certainly different from their
  own presuppositions. These need to be handled, to be unpacked and pupils need to try to make sense of them particularly in relation to their
  own views. This can be very hard and the teacher-facilitator may need to
  employ very specific question to help the process along.
- *Language*. As dialogue develops it requires an increasingly sophisticated
  use of language, a skill which for many pupils does not come naturally
  and has to be learned. This is not just the development of a religious
  vocabulary but learning how to communicate clearly, precisely and effectively.

– *Personal/social skills*. In the early stages of dialogue, pupils can find it hard how to handle disagreements without sulking or becoming angry or even hostile. Learning to cope with this is an important gift of dialogue!

In so many ways this is excellent practice especially in the hands of such expert practitioners as Ipgrave. In less experienced or informed hands it might not make the same rich contribution to religious understanding.

3. Perspectives

RE in England developed considerably in the last quarter of the twentieth century and has adjusted both its aims and content to meet the needs of an increasingly religiously plural society. In many ways it has both survived and to a certain degree thrived through adaptation!

The 1988 Education Reform Act which established the National Curriculum left RE in a rather unsatisfactory position. It was compulsory, it would be inspected, but unlike all the other subjects it was without a nationally defined content or assessment levels. It was different from the rest. It was required to be taught and it is clear from school inspection reports that after 1988 it was being taught much more extensively in primary schools. The main concern here was the variable quality of what was being taught.

Recent developments as we have seen, especially the National Framework for RE have enshrined the best practice and given a rationale for the subject, principles, an outline content and assessment levels. In addition the National Framework has received widespread endorsement in a very extensive consultation process. This is a major leap forward. At present the National Framework is non-statutory so in theory a local education authority could ignore it completely when its agreed syllabus has to be reviewed next. This is unlikely to happen in most cases. Many do hope that, especially as the National Framework is written in the format of a National Curriculum subject that the next step will be to make the Framework statutory so that RE can be a National Curriculum subject like all the rest.

References

Bastide, D. (1992) (Ed.) *Good Practice in Primary Religious Education* (London, Routledge).

Bastide, D. (1998) *Coordinating Religious Education Across the Primary School* (London, Routledge).

Bastide, D. (2006) *Teaching Religious Education 4-11* (London, Routledge).

Ipgrave, J. (2001) *Pupil-To-Pupil Dialogue in the Classroom as a Tool for Religious Education: Working Paper 2* (Warwick, Warwick Religious and Education Research Unit).

Ipgrave, J. (2003) *Building e-Bridges (Inter-faith dialogue by e-mail)* (Birmingham, RE Today Services, Christian Education Publications).

QCA (1998) *Exemplification of Standards for Religious Education* (London, QCA).

QCA (2000) *Religious Education: Non Statutory Guidance on RE* (London, QCA).

QCA (2004) *Religious Education: The Non Statutory National Framework* (London, QCA).

ERA (1988) http://www.opsi.gov.uk/ACTS/acts1988/Ukpga_19880040_en_2.htm
SCAA (1994) *The Model Syllabuses* (London, SCAA).
Schools' Council (1971) *Religious Education in the Secondary School* (London, Schools' Council).

Using Narratives in Primary Religious Education in Estonia*

Pille Valk and Olga Schihalejev

Introduction

Religious Education (RE) has an ambiguous position in the Estonian educational landscape. Though it has traditionally been a core school subject, dramatic changes in recent Estonian history, in particular the 50 years of Soviet occupation with its accompanying strong atheistic ideology, have led to a situation in which the place of the subject in the curriculum is one of the most debated topics in the country. RE could officially be resumed in Estonian schools after the Soviet occupation ended in 1991 (Valk, 2000:85). Nowadays it is taught in approximately 60 of the 600+ schools in the country, mostly at the primary and the upper secondary school level. The contested nature of RE underlines the need for a well-grounded concept of the subject in order to determine its identity in contemporary Estonia.

Our choice of an example of good practice in primary RE in Estonia is a particular approach to storytelling. For many centuries storytelling has been a classic means of transmitting religious knowledge, and recent developments in the fields of narrative theology and pedagogy have opened fresh perspectives and stimulated new thinking about the use of this method in today's schools.

1. Estonian School System, Primary Schools and Religious Education

The education system

In Estonia schooling is compulsory between the ages of 7-17 and is free for all who study in state-financed or municipal schools. The municipal authorities run the vast majority of schools, though there are a small number of private fee-paying schools. Pre-school education in crèches and kindergartens is followed by nine years of comprehensive education at basic school. Pupils pass through three stages: two at primary level and one at secondary (stage 1 years 1-3, stage 2 years 4-6, stage 3 years 7-9). Basic education is organised as a single structure that aims to ensure a smooth progression through the nine grades and an efficient transition between each stage. After basic school,

* The chapter presents part of a research project financed by Estonian Science Foundation grant 5839 (Theoretical and Practical Problems of Religious Education in Estonian Schools).

there are two pathways: 3 years continuation of secondary schooling in the gymnasium, or 3 or more years in vocational school.

National curricula set out a basic educational framework: the aims and objectives of schooling; the pedagogical basis for organising studies; mandatory and optional subjects; subject volume and curricular content; competencies expected of pupils; and grade descriptors, including the basic level of achievement expected of all school levers. Despite this central organisation each school prepares its own curriculum on the basis of the national curricula. Figure 1 gives an overview about the Estonian school system.

Figure 1: The Estonian school system

GYMNASIUM		IV school stage Age 15/16 - 18	12. Grade	VOCATIONAL EDUCATION
			11. Grade	
			10. Grade	
Compulsory BASIC SCHOOL		III school stage Age 12/13 – 15/16	9. Grade	
			8. Grade	
			7. Grade	
	Primary school	II school stage Age 9/10-12/13	6. Grade	
			5. Grade	
			4. Grade	
		I school stage Age 7 – 9/10	3. Grade	
			2. Grade	
			1. Grade	

The aims of schooling

The aims of education are established in the National Curricula. They were developed in the light of the Estonian and international legislative framework, political statements about education, scientific research, national and international experiences, and documents and recommendations provided by international organisations. There are four basic aims, to:
- develop Estonian national culture in a spirit of understanding and co-operation that supports the identities of other national groups living in Estonia, takes into consideration the European dimension, and promotes social integration
- promote the holistic development of the person
- enable pupils to flourish in the pluralistic and ever-changing world by developing the attitudes and skills necessary for cooperation and preparing them for life long learning
- support the development of the democratic society.

Religious Education

As we have already noted, RE has an ambiguous position in the educational landscape in Estonia. Many question the necessity for the subject in the curriculum. If religious educators are to resist such critical attacks they must establish a well-grounded concept of RE. To be meaningful, RE must be targeted: it has to address people's specific needs and expectations, deal with pupils' questions and problems, and take into consideration the particular nature of Estonian society. Understanding the context in which the subject will be delivered enables religious educators to develop a rationale for RE in a manner that integrates it into the broader education system and an appropriate choice of curriculum content and teaching methods. This is outlined in figure 2.

Figure 2: Outline of the model of contextual analysis

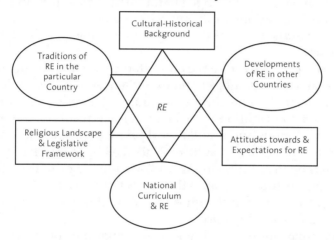

Such a contextual approach to RE in primary schools needs to take account of a number of important factors:

The historical and cultural background. Most parents of school-age children have no personal experiences from RE classes. Instead, their education was shaped during the years of Soviet occupation by a strong atheistic paradigm, which depicted religion as a cultural relic – an outmoded superstition that has no place in the modern scientific world. Thus, religious educators have to take into consideration the fact that many parents, pupils, teachers of other subjects and school principals lack even a basic knowledge of religious issues, and consequently often express opinions that are prejudicial against the subject. In this context the task of RE is to build bridges to Estonia's forgotten past by recovering the roots of the nation's cultural identity and linking it to the current concerns and questions of pupils.

The religious landscape and legislative framework. Most pupils have no church-related family background. According to the latest census, only 28% of Estonians acknowledged any religious affiliation (Census, 2000). Hence a plurality of worldviews constitutes an inescapable reality for RE to deal with. According to Estonian legislation, RE is an optional and non-confessional subject. It is up to parents to decide about the participation of their children in RE classes. Schools are obliged to organise RE classes whenever a minimum of 15 pupils at any given school stage request it. However, the structures to ensure that the law is fulfilled are often not in place. It is not clear, for example, whose responsibility it is to identify which pupils want to study the subject. In practice this means school principals are in a key position to decide whether or not RE is taught in their schools. They often identify obstacles to organising RE classes: e.g. limited timetable space, lack of interest on the part of pupils, or the absence of qualified teachers. RE teachers are required to have both theological and pedagogical training. The lack of trained teachers is a serious problem, and frequently undermines attempts to provide RE lessons. Because it is an optional subject, RE is not subject to central inspection.

Attitudes towards RE. Despite the contested nature of the subject, research into attitudes towards the subject and expectations about what it might provide pupils, indicated some common ground. There is widespread agreement that it has a contribution to make to moral education, the understanding of different religions and secular worldviews, and the exploration of the interface between religion and culture (Valk, 2003). Research in the spring of 2004, conducted by Pille Valk amongst 187 parents of primary school pupils, shed light on the attitudes towards the subject of parents whose children attend RE lessons. Answers to the question 'Why did you send your children to RE classes?' included the following:
  – to broaden their outlook on life – as a normal part of education it helps them understand different cultures
  – to help them to see things from different perspectives
  – to respond to their interest in RE
  – to develop their moral and spiritual education
  – to learn something they had missed when they attended school.

It is interesting to note that these parents rejected the main criticism of the subject presented in media debates, namely that RE involves brainwashing and proselytising.

The history of RE in Estonia. The creation of the national school system of the newly-born independent state of Estonia at the beginning of the 1920s was accompanied by a fundamental reform in the teaching of RE (Valk, 1997; Valk & Lehtsaar, 2003). There is space here only to identify some of the key features of this reform:

- a clear distinction was made between catechesis in the Church and RE in the school, marking the beginning of the non-confessional approach in contemporary schools
- RE became an optional subject
- a children-centred approach was adopted, in which the learning objects of the subject were linked to the lifeworlds of pupils and attempts were made to respond to their personal questions and concerns
- the subject was closely related to moral education, and the need to integrate RE with the other school subjects recognised
- amongst methodological recommendations at the primary level, particular emphasis was placed on the value of good lively storytelling.

The international context. In the present context the emergence in many different countries of a 'new wave' of narrative teaching methods is especially significant. In particular, the work of the Finnish religious educator Pertti Luumi has had a major impact on the development of these methods in Estonia (Luumi, 1987). We will return to this issue in the second part of the chapter.

Links between RE and national curricula. It is important to see the subject in the context of the whole landscape of schooling, and especially in the light of the common ground between RE and the fields of moral education and cultural studies. Learning about and learning from religious traditions can contribute to mutual respect and understanding between different people, while religious literacy creates the conditions for better understanding of topics explored by other subjects, such as literature, history, music and art.

The RE curriculum

The most recent version of the RE curriculum was developed on the basis of a contextual analysis. The basic principles guiding the pedagogy of the subject are that teaching must respect human rights, the freedom of religious belief and individual conscience. Rather than seeking to proselytise, teachers must resist forms of fundamentalism, discrimination and intolerance and strive instead to promote dialogue and mutual understanding between different worldviews. As such, the subject has an important contribution to make to moral and value education. Given the deep impact of religions in culture – literature, music, art etc. –, it is recognised that religious understanding is a necessary precondition for understanding the world's cultural heritage.

The curriculum identifies the main aims of RE as the:
- provision of knowledge about different religions, worldviews and cultures as a means towards religious literacy that can provide a key to understanding cultural heritage

- creation of an open identity, i.e. one in which pupils understand their own culture and the culture of others in a manner that provides the basis for mutual understanding and tolerance
- expansion of religious literacy as a precondition to dialogue, in order to help overcome national and religious conflicts
- recognition and evaluation of spiritual values
- establishment of critical attitudes towards mass culture and consumerism
- growth of social and ecological awareness and responsibility
- formation of pupils' moral development
- promotion of the skills necessary for making responsible choices and developing one's own worldview.

Curriculum development in a context where some schools offer RE only in the first grades and some only in gymnasium, and where there are very few schools with RE in all grades is inevitably a complicated undertaking. Currently attempts to meet these challenges take the form of a syllabus that contains both 'core' and 'optional' courses. The system is described in figure 3.

Figure 3: Structure of the syllabus

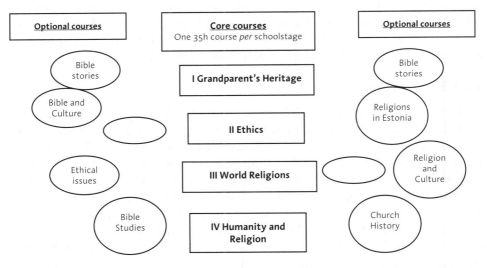

Though core courses have a detailed and determined content, teachers and pupils may still work together to design 20% of their content. This makes it possible to take better account of pupils' concerns and the local context. In designing optional courses teachers have even more freedom: the basic principles and main aims establish the frame of such courses, but the material content is left for teachers and pupils to negotiate between themselves. And indicated with the empty circles in figure 2, the list of the possible optional courses remains open.

The primary school syllabus consists of two core courses. The first, 'Grandparent's Heritage', contains four main topics: the wonder of life and holiness, festivals and traditions, selected stories from the Bible, and values and moral education. Among the available teaching methods, special attention is paid to storytelling, creative activities and the development of concentration skills. The teacher's task is to create a supportive and secure atmosphere in the lessons in order to sustain the pupils' personal development. The second, 'Ethics', focuses on three topics: the Decalogue, the classical virtues and the 'Golden Rule'. These are illustrated by three sorts of resources: stories from the religious traditions, stories about outstanding people (e.g. Albert Schweitzer, Mother Theresa, Mahatma Gandhi and the Dalai Lama), and significant stories from everyday life in which values are a live issue (*Médecins Sans Frontières*, voluntary work with people in need etc). Teaching methods seek to explore moral dilemmas through discussion, value clarification and analyses. Pedagogical suggestions emphasise storytelling and active learning methods such as group-work, discussion, role-play and project work.

2. Methods and Examples of Good Practice

Many centuries ago, a rich sultan in Baghdad gave a banquet in honour of the birth of his son. All the nobility who partook of the fest brought costly gifts, except a young sage who came empty-handed. He explained to the sultan, 'Today the young prince will receive many precious gifts, jewels and rare coins. My gift is different. From the time he is old enough to listen until manhood, I will come to the palace every day and tell him stories of our Arabian heroes. When he becomes our ruler he will be just and honest.' The young sage kept his word. When the prince was at last made sultan, he became famous for his wisdom and honour. To this day, an inscription on a scroll in Baghdad reads, 'It was because of the seed sown by the tales' (Bausch, 1984:50).

Reviewing the teaching methods utilised in primary religious education in Estonia, both now and in the past, it is not surprising that we decided to choose storytelling for the closer attention. Why? The method has much to offer in our specific context, where there are very few tailor-made teaching and learning resources available and teachers often have to respond to the challenge of 'making something out of nothing'. Developing the skills of story writing and telling provides a wonderfully creative methodological tool for teachers which they can use in many different ways and circumstances. And last but not least – children love stories!

It is impossible to give an exhaustive presentation of the many issues surrounding storytelling in this chapter. Fortunately there is a broad variety of the literature about the topic (Zipes, 1997; Loughlin, 1999; Shaw, 1999; Shank, 2000; Salans, 2004; Yust, 2006). Here we will concentrate only on the main theoretical outlines and provide some practical examples. We will focus on Bible stories, specifically on the re-telling of Bible stories through the eyes of the main character.

The theoretical background

Narrative is a very basic way by which people experience, understand, and act in the world. As a seemingly universal human characteristic, narrative ability offers religious educators a profound means through which to facilitate the desired goals of RE. Stories can touch, challenge, and change learners on cognitive, affective, and behavioural levels as they are used effectively within religious instruction (Shaw, 1999:4).

This quotation, taken from Susan Shaw's fascinating and comprehensive study *Storytelling in Religious Education*, identifies some key reasons why storytelling is important in RE.

Stories are acts of experience, expression, and recognition (Sayers, 1969: 86). From experience, storytellers construct narratives that imbue events with meaning. The resultant story then becomes a cognitive, affective, and behavioural experience for those who hear it, as they recognise themselves in the story. In other words, storytellers render their experience in the story, and, if the story is true to human experience, learners find themselves participating in the story as well (Shaw, 1999:53). Stories, therefore, are an experiential learning process, involving cognitive, affective, and behavioural modes of learning. They explain humans to themselves, not by describing truth about the external world but by creating and recreating experiential truths in people's lives (56).

Psychologist Jerome Bruner has suggested that cognition is characterised by two modes of thought, which he has labelled 'propositional' and 'narrative' thinking (Bruner, 1986; 1996). Propositional thinking is logical, analytical, and abstract, while narrative thinking is imaginative, intuitive, and concrete. Narrative thinking allows people to make sense of their experiences and to understand the world. At the same time, particularly in the context of primary RE, stories have an important role to play in the cognitive domain of learning. They help learners store, retain, and recall information, and more importantly can help pupils to move beyond mere information to new ideas and deeper understanding. Stories stimulate the imagination and encourage creativity. In fact, research indicates that children who do not hear stories during their early years can suffer deprivation of both mind and spirit (Fransworth, quoted in Shaw 1999:120). Pupils who engage with stories learn to value process, attitudes and lifestyles, develop imagination, communication skills, and critical thinking, and come to appreciate diversity and integration (Shaw, 1999:121). These basic skills are essential components of the self-directed learners that RE seeks to develop. For the teacher, storytelling is an important tool for achieving a myriad of educational objectives.

Stories in the Judaeo-Christian tradition

Hear, O Israel! The LORD is our God, the LORD is one! You shall love the LORD your God with all your heart and with all your soul and with all your might. These words, which I am commanding you today, shall be on your heart. You shall teach them diligently to your sons and shall talk of them when you sit in your house and when you walk by the way and when you lie down and when you rise up (Deut 6:4ff,) (New American Standard Bible).

The Sch'ma (Jewish Prayer) recognises the importance of teaching God's covenant story diligently to Jewish children. For Christians, the story of God's acts in human history continues in the Christ-story of the New Testament and in the stories of the Christian community across the centuries. It is interesting to note, that almost half of the Hebrew scripture and two-thirds of the New Testament are narrative texts (Luumi, 1987:85ff). All the central motifs of the Christian faith – creation, the fall, incarnation etc. – are presented as stories. When the disciples asked Jesus 'Who is our neighbour?' he did not reply with a definition of neighbourliness, but instead he told a story. The task of the religious educator is to build bridges between the Bible stories and the pupils. This goal is significant in all forms of RE, both in confessional and non-confessional approaches. It is the core of learning about and from religion.

The most familiar types of stories used in RE are those that take place in 'Bible times'. In the approach to storytelling presented here, the retelling stays close to the biblical version but may be retold from the 'main character's' point of view. This main character might be one of the characters appearing in the biblical account, or a fictional character who is imagined to have been present at the time. We present a practical example of this approach later in the chapter.

It is also possible to create a 'frame story' which places the biblical story in a wider interpretative context and opens up a wide range of learning opportunities. Here the 'frame' of the story may take place in ancient times or may start in a contemporary context. Thus, a story of a contemporary moral dilemma may include within it the retelling of the Bible story.

Preparing a story

Religious educators can prepare to use a story in a lesson by analysing it in order to arrive at a deeper understanding. Such analysis can also offer helpful glues about appropriate uses of dialogue, movement and props in the process of retelling. The more teachers understand a story and are aware of its dynamics, the more effective they will be in communicating it (Shaw, 1999:15).

The following scheme offers a tool for analysing Bible stories and draws – with some supplements – on the work of Luumi (Luumi, 1987:21). We name this tool the 'PTPTAM analysis'.

People – the characters of the story. Who participates? Who is mentioned in the text? Whom can pupils imagine as other participants, connected somehow to the story (men, women or children with different backgrounds)? What do we know about the situation of the participants from Bible or from secondary literature? What, for example, does it mean to be blind? How was blindness understood in biblical times? What are the relationships between the characters? Which social and religious attitudes are implied in the story: tax collectors as collaboraters, Samaritans as impure, Pharisees as a moral elite? From all the participants, one character has to be chosen as the main character of the story – the one through whose eyes the story will be told. A good choice of main character gives pupils the opportunity to walk in his or her shoes.

Terms – the critical vocabulary in the story. Not all terms will be familiar to pupils. Measures may need explaining. How much wine was made out of water in wedding festival in Cana? Hundreds of litres! How high was the golden statue erected by Nebuchadnezzar that the brave Jewish men refused to worship? About the height of a ten-story building! The same is true for the value of money. What could be obtained for a lepton, the smallest coin? If a denari, the usual fee for a day's work, was enough to pay for a family's daily living expenses, and a talent was equal to approximately 6,000 denari, imagine what it mean to be in debt to the tune of 10,000 talents! So, also for distances: the journey from Nazareth to Bethlehem undertaken by Mary and Joseph is about 120 km! The storyteller must explain such terms to pupils and enable them to understand and imagine their significance.

Place – the environment in which the events take place. Some places had a special meaning. The temple in Jerusalem is the religious centre for Jews, the most holy place within the most holy city, while Samaria is the country of infidels, heretics and outcasts. Pupils need to know about the nature of these places, about everyday life and the occupations of people, and the outlooks of various communities.

Time – the chronological frame of story. When did the action take place, and over what period of time? Certain times and feasts had often a special meaning: healing on the Sabbath contravenes the Torah, and Jesus was cruci-fied during Passover.

Action – What is going on in the story? In what order do the events oc-cur? Who says what and to whom? What does Jesus say? What does he do? Is there anything special or unexpected (the fact that Jesus spoke with a Samaritan woman would have been a scandal in Jewish society)? How do people react? Why? Thus the plot of the story needs to be identified or cre-ated. Most plots of stories have a basic outline: a beginning, introducing the main character and the problem that needs resolving; a series of events that gradually build up the tension of the narrative as it moves towards a crisis point (a good storyteller never reveals the outcome at the beginning, because this only destroys the tension); the resolution of the story, which often comes as a surprise to the listener; and finally the conclusion or 'coming down'.

Message – the meaning of the story. Pupils need to identify the 'most im-portant thing' in the story: the key idea that the teacher wants to convey. One story may have many possible interpretations, depending on the vari-ous intentions, storytellers, listeners and contexts. Each interpretation may have some validity, but each will lead to a different way of adapting and communicating the story. Hence, choosing the 'most important thing' for the particular lesson should be closely tied to the desired learning outcomes. It is also important to consider how to make the chosen aspect relevant to the contemporary situation and the questions children ask. It is important that storytellers keep in mind the fact that a good story explains itself in the plot. Naïve narrow moralising by the storyteller will destroy the richness of the story. It is important that pupils have the opportunity to share their interpre-tations, feelings, and reactions.

There are some practical issues that we recommend teachers to consider be-fore telling the stories in the classroom.

Storytelling is a special time in the lesson. Whenever possible we suggest sitting pupils in a circle. This makes it easier for the storyteller to make eye contact with the listeners, follow their reactions, and so help them to 'get into story'. Storytelling could take place in a special area of the classroom: sitting down on the 'storytelling carpet' or pillows may create an appropriate at-mosphere and so help pupils to concentrate on the story. As far as possible, external distractions should be avoided.

When telling a story, a good storyteller uses short sentences. Primary at-tention has to be given to the verbs, since they create the dynamic of the story. Avoid using too many adjectives as these can deflect from the tension. A good tempo helps retain pupils' attention: too fast and the story is impos-sible to follow, too slow and it becomes boring. Clear diction and sensitive use of pauses can benefit pupils' comprehension. Skilful use of intonation can make the story more vivid, though over-emotional or naïve intonation is undesirable. A good storyteller invites children to engage with all the senses: not only listening, but also seeing, smelling, touching and even tasting! Sometimes it is helpful to introduce some aids to the storytelling, such as simple puppets or pictures, especially when the pupils have difficulties to concentrate, could be used in such cases. Use of sound effects – knocking, whistling etc. –, and gestures may also be effective.

Every teacher can learn the skills of storytelling. It is often asked whether it is best to tell the story or read from a book: we recommend direct telling, though if the teacher is insecure then it can be better simply to read it.

A Practical Example: The Story of Bartimaeus

Using the PTPTAM analyses provides RE teacher with powerful tool with which to approach the telling of Bible stories in the classroom. Here we present a practical example of its use in a lesson about the healing of Bartimaeus:

> Then they came to Jericho And as He was leaving Jericho with His disciples and a large crowd, a blind beggar named Bartimaeus, the son of Timaeus, was sitting by the road. When he heard that it was Jesus the Nazarene, he began to cry out and say, 'Jesus, Son of David, have mercy on me!' Many were sternly telling him to be quiet, but he kept crying out all the more,' Son of David, have mercy on me!' And Jesus stopped and said, 'Call him here.' So they called the blind man, saying to him, 'Take courage, stand up! He is calling for you.' Throwing aside his cloak, he jumped up and came to Jesus. And answering him, Jesus said, 'What do you want Me to do for you?' And the blind man said to Him, 'Rabboni, I want to regain my sight!' And Jesus said to him, 'Go; your faith has made you well.' Immediately he regained his sight and began following Him on the road (Mk 10:46ff) (New American Standard Bible).

Preparation of the narrative: PTPTAM analyses

People – The *blind man* suffers from a disease that was thought to be a punishment from God for sin. The miracle is also described in Matthew's and Luke's Gospels (Mtt 20:29ff, Lk 18:35ff), but here it is more personalised: the blind man has a name that points to his origin (Bartimaeus, or bar-Timaeus the son of Timaeus) and his anguish is described most vividly – he is desperate, crying out for help and unconcerned that in doing so he is annoying other people. Mark's Gospel portrays the *disciples* as spiritually blind, since despite Jesus' teaching they still do not understand who he is: in their 'blindness' they scold the blind man for bothering Jesus, but then start to 'see' and help Bartimaeus to come to him. Jesus is travelling with other *pilgrims* to the Festival of Passover in Jerusalem, and is also surrounded by *inhabitants of Jericho*. Usually a rabbi would teach people during the journey: evidently so did Jesus, but the blind man's cry disturbs the crowd's festal mood and makes it difficult for them to hear what Jesus is saying. It is highly likely that there were children among his audience. Choosing a child as the 'main character' helps pupils to get into the story: here we have taken a boy, whom we have named 'Ben'.

Terms – When Bartimaeus speaks to Jesus he uses the Aramaic word *Rabbouni*, which means *teacher* and has connotations of respect. However, and of far greater importance for the story, in his agony he also refers to Jesus as the *Son of David*: a Messianic title that expresses all the political and religious hopes of the Jewish nation. He believes Jesus to be the Messiah, and according to ancient prophecy he has good reason to ask for help since when the Messiah comes 'the eyes of the blind shall be opened' (Isa 35:5). Significantly, Jesus accepts the title of Messiah.

Place – Jericho is one of the lowest-situated towns in the whole world, lying beside the river Jordan north of the Dead Sea and 22 km northeast from Jerusalem. It is on the pilgrimage route from Galilee, six hours journey from Jerusalem. The town is one of the oldest towns in the world, established in 7,000 B.C., and was originally a fortress city. It has a spring that makes it an oasis in the desert; in the Old Testament it is referred to as the 'city of palms' (Deut 34:3, 2 Chr 28:15 et. al.). When the people of Israel came to conquer the land of Canaan, Jericho was the first obstacle in their path (Josh 2). In the time of Elijah and Elisha the city was the hometown of several prophets (2 Kings 2). Jericho is mentioned in the New Testament on a number of occasions: the healing of Bartimaeus (Mt 20:29, Mk 10:46, Lk 18:35), the parable of the Good Samaritan (Lk 10:30), and the story of Zacchaeus (Lk 19:1).

Time – According to all three synoptic Gospels Jericho was the last place Jesus stopped at before entering Jerusalem a few days before his death. Jesus has already foretold his suffering, but many people including his disciples saw him as a victorious political redeemer rather than as God's suffering servant. Bartimaeus cries out the secret hope of disciples – that he is David's Son, the Messiah, who will go up to Jerusalem to restore David's Kingdom and inaugurate a new Golden Age.

Action – Jesus and his disciples go out of Jericho; the blind man is sitting in the street and cries out to Jesus; he is told to be quiet, but cries out even more; Jesus stands still and calls Bartimaeus to him; the blind man throws off his coat and comes; Jesus asks a question, the blind man answers – and is cured!; he joins Jesus on his journey.

Message – There are many levels of meaning in the story, and hence many possible 'most important things'. Teachers must select the meaning most appropriate to the learning objectives. In our story the accent is on the importance of faith and compassion.

Our Story: Ben's Special Day

Ben screwed up his brown eyes to protect them from the dazzling sunshine. He pushed forward up the hill and wiped the sweat from his forehead. Every time he wanted to leave the town, he had to go upwards, because the town lay in a valley. But today it wasn't too hard. Why? He was rushing to meet his new friend! He was really happy that he had found a good companion with whom he could speak about important things. But... his new friend couldn't see: nothing at all – he was blind. It was so interesting, so different to hear, when he explained how he recognised things by smell and touch, how he learnt to walk around and cope with everyday life. Ben hadn't thought about such things before. Talking with Bartimaeus, Ben discovered a new world, one much more interesting than anything he had imagined before. But it was difficult, even impossible, to describe some simple and obvious things to his new friend. Once Ben told about the blue sky, and suddenly Bartimaeus interrupted by asking 'What is blue?' How to explain such things to a blind man?

But there was something else that troubled Ben in this friendship. Ben couldn't speak about it to his other friends. Ben's father has always taught that a man deserves what he gets. If the person is blind, there has to be a reason, it has to be God's punishment for their sins. Ben knew also that one must try to keep apart from both sin and sinner. But his new friend was blind. And how could he explain to others that he, a ten year old boy, is the friend of a blind man?

Still Ben was anxious to meet his friend and towards the road leading to Jerusalem. He was sure that his friend was there. Usually Bartimaeus sat by the town gates, begging and hoping for some charity from merciful people. Although he wasn't loved, sometimes a small amount of money was given to him. There were many people on the streets today. The Passover was coming and Ben knew that many people want to go to Jerusalem, to the Holy City, for this most important holiday. 'Hopefully it is not too crowded and we can talk', Ben thought to himself.

Ben approached the town gates. Turning the corner, he saw a huge crowd. 'Why are there so many people? Maybe I can see some famous rabbi with his followers? But what about my friend: will they give anything to him? What if they only blame him for his blindness?' Ben felt pain in his heart. Then, suddenly he realised: 'What will it matter if somebody sees me talking with a blind beggar?' He moved forward...

Ben heard the voice of Bartimaeus: 'Jesus, Son of David, have mercy on me!' Ben hurried up. 'Who is the man Bartimaeus called in that way? The Son of David is supposed to be the Messiah! God himself has spoken through the prophets and foretold that one day He will send a redeemer, the Messiah. Has that powerful warrior come with his army to cast away the Romans from our country?' Ben forgot all decency and elbowed his way through the crowd. He wants to see!

Bartimaeus was still crying. Ben heard grumbling: 'What are you doing blind man, annoying respectful people? You are disturbing us! Be quiet!' People came between the rabbi and Bartimaeus to try to stop him disturbing their festal mood.

Ben heard Bartimaeus voice. It was even louder than before: 'Have mercy on me, Son of David!' Ben felt embarrassed that his friend did not listen to what people were saying to him. But then he heard a firm, calm: 'Call him!' The rabbi people called Jesus had stopped talking and stood still. A murmur went through the crowd.

They took Bartimaeus to be a disturber, but now Jesus himself was calling him! So they called the blind man and said to him: 'Have courage! Get up. He's calling for you'. Ben saw clearly Bartimaeus jumping up for joy, throwing off his beggar's coat and walking with hands outstretched towards the voice of Jesus. He was amazingly fast and steady. People stepped back and made way for him. Ben looked at Jesus. He wasn't much like a warrior, but he radiated peace and kindness. Jesus asked Bartimaeus: 'What do you want me to do for you?' In Ben's mind's eye appeared all the dreams Bartimaeus had talked about: many supporting friends, a small work-shop, a cosy home, a family – a wife and at least seven healthy sons ...

But Bartimaeus said simply: 'Rabbouni, I want to see!' 'Go your way,' Jesus told him 'Your faith has healed you'. In an instant Ben was next to Bartimaeus and grasp-ing his rough hand. He understood that his blind friend saw something what no one else could see: Jesus was not only a rabbi, but he was the Messiah with the power to help him. Ben squeezed his friend's hand and looked at him. He saw the clear and cheerful look of Bartimaeus as he looked around at the people, at Ben and then up at the sky. 'It's blue,' whispered Ben, feeling that he had said something extremely important.

Examples for further work

Role play

Groups prepare an episode from the life of Bartimaeus:
  - Bartimaeus on a street before the meeting with Jesus; there are many peo-ple passing; show their different attitudes towards Bartimaeus.
  - Bartimaeus meets his relatives after the healing – What did they say to each other? What they think about the miracle?

Art

Pupils respond to the story by:
  - Drawing a picture of all the colours and wonderful things Bartimaeus could see after the healing.
  - Dividing the story into episodes (Bartimaeus sitting by the gate and beg-ging, Jesus and his disciples approaching the city gates, Bartimaeus cry-ing out to Jesus, etc.) and groups create a picture about each episode; when completed, the pictures are glued together into scroll, the ends are attached to a stick, and the 'ancient book' is ready to be used as a visual aid when it is time to tell the story again.

3. Perspectives

RE in Estonian schools is in an ambivalent situation: on the one hand there is legislation that makes the subject available, but a lot of work has to be done to develop the concept of RE suitable for its position in a post-socialist society; on the other hand RE as an optional subject forced to struggle with many problems, not least the suspicion and ignorance directed towards it.

Two key preconditions requiring support from the government for future positive developments are:
- The creation of a clear and effective legislative framework to guarantee the stability and status of the subject.
- Developments in teacher training: both a specialist training to prepare motivated and professionally skilled teachers for *all* schools, and the inclusion of the subject in the curricula of all teacher training programs in order to widen the outlook of all teachers in religious issues, support the adequate treatment of religion in other school subjects, and help overcome prejudices and ignorance.

On the other hand, legislative framework alone can not solve all the problems. Good everyday practice in teaching RE is needed as well. From this point of view, one can emphasise the following:
- RE teachers have to find creative ways to build bridges between religious traditions and the lives of nowadays pupils' who are mostly alienated from any religious tradition, and often come from the secularised background, and
- to build these bridges in a way that helps pupils to discover the richness of these traditions for themselves.

Storytelling is one of the possibilities that might provide means to achieve these challenging objectives.

References

Bausch, W. J. (1984) *Storytelling: Imagination and Faith, Mystic* (Connecticut, Twenty-Third Publications).

Bruner, J. (1986) *Actual Minds, Possible Worlds* (Cambridge, Massachusetts, Harvard University Press).

Bruner, J. (1996) *The Culture of Education* (Cambridge, Massachusetts, Harvard University Press).

Census (2000) *Population and Housing Census IV* (Tallinn, Statistikaamet).

Luumi, P. (1987) *Taitava Kertoja* (Helsinki, Painokaari OY).

Sayers, D. (1969) *The Whimsical Christian* (New York, Macmillan).

Loughlin, G. (1999) *Telling God's Story: Bible, Church and Narrative Theology* (New York, Cambridge University Press).

Salans, M. (2004) *Storytelling with Children in Crisis* (Jessica Kingsley Publishers).

Shank, R. (2000) *Tell Me a Story* (Northwestern University Press).

Shaw, S. M. (1999) *Storytelling in Religious Education* (Birmingham, Alabama, Religious Education Press).

Valk, P. (1997) *Ühest heledast laigust Eesti kooli ajaloos [RE in Estonian Schools 1918-1940]* (Tallinn, Logos).

Valk, P. (2000) From the Soviet Atheism to the National Identity: a Specific Background for the Religious Education in Estonia, *Panorama. International Journal of Comparative Religious Education and Values,* 12 (1), 78-93.

Valk, P. (2002). *Eesti kooli religiooniõpetuse kontseptsioon [The Concept of RE for Estonian Schools]* (Tartu, Tartu Ülikooli kirjastus).

Valk, P. (2003) 'Religious Education through the Eyes of Pupils, Teachers and Headmasters', in: M. Dietrich & T. Kulmar (Eds.) *Die Bedeutung der Religion für Gesellschaften in Vergangenheit und Gegenwart* (Münster, Ugarit-Verlag), 239-252.

Valk, P. & Lehtsaar, T. (2003) Developments of Practical Theology in Today's Estonia, *International Journal of Practical Theology*, 7 (1), 101-130.

Yust, K. M. (2006) *Nurturing Child and Adolescent Spirituality*. Perspectives from the World's Religious Traditions (Rowman & Littlefield Publishers).

Zipes, J. (1997) *Creative Storytelling: Building Community, Changing Lives* (New York, Routledge).

'Godly Play' – a Method of Storytelling in Finnish Schools

Sari Nevalainen and Juha Luodeslampi

Introduction

The Institute for RE in Finland supports primary school teachers in their pedagogical needs regarding RE. Part of its mandate is to research new methods and provide in-service training for teachers. *Godly Play* has recently been adopted as one of the methods for further development. It has roots in parish education but can be adapted and adjusted for use in the school.

Mainstream Finnish cultural heritage is rooted in the Lutheran tradition and in the modern Nordic lifestyle. This specific cultural background requires cultural adaptation in pedagogical methods.

The Bible and especially its narratives are essential parts of teaching RE at primary level. A large number of teachers experience pedagogical problems because their own knowledge of the Bible or their own attitudes about religion are insufficient to be a basis for teaching. This aspect calls for supportive training. The methods used should be easily understood at practical level.

The Institute for RE has compiled practical experiences with *Godly Play*. The method seems to fit well into the curricula and shows benefits in classroom practice.

1. Education System, Primary School and Religious Education

Pre-school teaching is provided at schools and day-care centres. Pre-school teaching covers the year before children start comprehensive school. The aim is to improve children's capacity for school and learning. In practice, children are taught mainly through play. Participation in pre-school is voluntary.

Children start school at the age of 7. It is possible to start school one year earlier or later based on an evaluation of the physical and mental development of the child. In Finland schooling is compulsory for nine years. 10-year comprehensive schools are normally run by the local authorities. The government contributes to the financing of all schools.

Figure 1: The Finnish school system

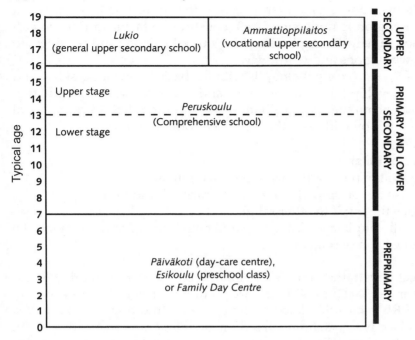

Only few private schools exist in Finland. Most schools are not based on religion or supported by a religious community. There are less than 15 Christian schools and a few other faith-based schools in the country. For children, schooling and educational supplies are provided free of charge.

The schools can develop individual profiles by focusing on a specific area. This can be e.g. languages, mathematics and sciences, sports, music or arts. Completing the basic education syllabus fulfils compulsory education. In Finland, 99.7% of each age cohort currently complete compulsory schooling.

Religious Education in Finnish schools

During the first six years, the class teacher, who is responsible for all or most subjects, also teaches RE. Instruction in the upper secondary school (three years) is usually organised in separate subjects, with specialised teachers for different subjects. Basic education also includes pupil counselling and, if necessary, special education.

In Finland there are no inspections within the school system. The local municipality (*kunta*) is responsible for the quality of teaching and where problems develop the national board of education can intervene in a consultative role.

In RE, the religious dimension of life is addressed from the perspective of the pupil's own development and seen in the context of broader social phenomena. Religion is understood as a constitutive factor in Finnish culture. Education in religion emphasises religious knowledge and readiness to encounter new religions and worldviews.

The task of RE is to equip the pupils with the basic knowledge, skills, and experience to develop their own identity and world-view. The instruction is intended to encourage and facilitate exploring the religious and ethical dimension of one's own life and the life of the community.

The objectives of RE are:
- to familiarise the pupil with his or her own religion
- to familiarise the pupil with the Finnish spiritual tradition
- to introduce the pupil to other religions
- to educate the pupil in ethical living and help him or her understand the ethical dimension of religion.

The first objective is rather simple in Finland. Based on the fact that 84.1% (as of 31 December 2003) of all Finns are members of the Lutheran church, the content of RE is mostly related to the Lutheran tradition. The basic idea behind this objective is defining freedom of religion as a positive right. Everyone has the right to RE, not just the (negative) right to not be confronted with a world view. This position takes special account of the situation of minority religious groups in the country.

Universal religious education is oriented towards majority beliefs. In the Finnish context this is Lutheran. All pupils may participate in this subject, but they can opt out at the request of their legal guardians. This legal option is rarely used. The main problems concern small Christian denominations. That is why many non-Lutheran pupils are studying Lutheran RE. Education in other religions will be provided if there is a minimum of three pupils who belong to a religion that is officially registered in Finland. Religious education is a compulsory subject both in comprehensive schools (7-16 years) and in upper secondary schools (16-18/19 years).

The point of Lutheran instruction is to introduce the pupils to religious culture from many perspectives and develop the major factors from the point of view of the pupils' development. RE helps the pupils understand the meaning of religion to individuals and to see the influence religions exert in society and culture. The objective is a broad general education in religion and in individual identity formation.

The core task of education about Lutheran religion in the first five grades is to offer material that supports the further development of the pupil's worldview. RE introduces the pupils to their religious environment by providing knowledge and by taking into consideration their own experiences, by making them familiar with the Bible, and by encouraging them to exercise responsibility and ethical judgement.

The Finnish Orthodox Church is growing in numbers. It has now 55,000 members, which is 1.1% of the Finnish population. The Catholic Church has a membership of around 8,000. The membership of other Protestant denominations such as Baptists, Methodists, the Salvation Army and Adventists is under 1% of the population. The number of Jews is about 1,000. About 80-90% of Finns state that the opportunity to have their children baptised, to get married in church and to have a church funeral are important reasons for church membership.

The issue of 'Confession' in Religious Education

Finnish RE was confessionally organised on a Sunday school model to nurture children in the Lutheran faith up to the 1940s. After 1946 the concept of 'confessional' changed its meaning. The idea was not to foster allegiance but to choose material based on the confessional majority. In Finland this means mainly Lutheran. Confessional religious education in terms of content meant teaching about the Bible and Lutheran ethics at the primary school level. During late 1960s and early 1970s the atheistic movement was strong and the idea of a pedagogical understanding of 'confessional' was made clearer. Teachers were allowed to present stories and issues but they were not allowed to express their own confession. A widespread slogan of that time was that RE had as much to do with confession as mathematics (Saine, 2000).

The concept 'according to one's own religion' is rather new since RE was defined as denominational before 2003. However, during the last two decades, Finnish Lutheran denominational RE has been understood as non-confessional in spiritual or religious terms. The term 'confessional' only indicates the content of the subject. This was primarily knowledge about one's own religion. Religious education understood this way differs from religious practice. Basically, the concept of 'one's own religion' is an updated version of recent good practice.

Religious education is a compulsory subject in both comprehensive schools (7-16 years) and in senior/upper secondary schools (16-18/19 years).

Over the past 30 years, the interpretation of the term 'confessional' as applied to RE has posed problems in view of the change in its meaning. For example, if the content of RE in primary school is Bible stories, this could be interpreted in many ways as confessional. This has led to a debate on whether the pedagogies of RE should be developed towards encouraging the pupil's own reflection and nourish an open atmosphere.

The final push to reject the word 'confessional' for RE was the recent Act for Religious Freedom (2003). The previous law established freedom from religion. The current law, on the contrary, is based on the concept of a positive right: freedom for religion. In this context, the confessional and denominational basis of RE were ambiguous and problematic terms, and the simple solution was to legislate current good practice.

The main aim of Lutheran religious education in Finland is to make the students more aware of their own religious culture. Teaching is always tailored to the students' age and maturity. RE helps students to understand the meaning of religion to individuals and to see how religion influences society and culture. The objective is a broad general education in religion as well as understanding religion at a personal level.

2. Methods and Example of Good Practice

Religious education in primary school is based on Bible stories. In recent years, the narrative approach has become very popular in pedagogies centred on the Bible. The major problem of this methodology is that it depends on the teacher's personal storytelling skills. Some can do it, but others can not. The method of *Godly Play* provides clear and effective guidelines for telling stories. Almost everyone can learn it. The wonderful innovation of that method, in pedagogical terms, is the creative responsive work after stories. *Godly Play* is seen as rather open and safe by teachers. It largely excludes the possibility of religious indoctrination and should support open discussion (Kosunen & Luodeslampi, 2005).

Godly Play is a special Bible-story telling method developed by Dr. Jerome Berryman over 30 years. He studied Montessori pedagogy in the 1960´s and came across Sofia Cavaletti's method, which is based on storytelling using different types of wooden figures. Berryman's idea was to develop Cavaletti's method by his own lights. The process has been very much based on testing it with children. It is thus safe to say that *Godly Play* concentrates on children's ways of understanding (www.godlyplay.org).

It is an approach to children's spiritual development that is based on creating a sacred space in which to present the stories of our faith, wonder about them together, and then allow the children, usually with the aid of art supplies, to engage with the story on their own terms. The method is rooted in the Christian tradition, but at the same time open to new ideas and creativity.

The stories are told in a simple manner and without further interpretation or moral instruction. When a story is presented, the children and the storyteller wonder together about the aspects of the story that draw their interest. After some time spent exploring the story, it is put away and the children are free to choose the art supplies they would like to work with. They spend some time creating whatever they choose, in response to what they feel is the most important or interesting aspect of the story. After this, it is time for a joint celebration – which usually means a glass of milk and a cookie.

There are three kinds of basic story categories: parables, sacred stories and liturgical stories. All stories include special material made of wood and textiles. Detailed manuscripts including gestures, a story line and wondering questions have been developed for each story. The Montessorian approach to education has been adapted to *Godly Play* in order to stimulate children's active participation in story and ritual and to awaken their creativity.

Godly Play is usually used with children in the context of Sunday school or in church day clubs. It is widely practised in the Church of Finland. *Godly Play* is connected to another larger project in the Finnish Lutheran church. The project is known as Church at Play. The idea in this project or approach is to take a more holistic approach to education in situations where the church relates to children. The widespread adoption of *Godly Play* was based on the need for this kind of method in the larger context of this project (Kosunen & Luodeslampi, 2005).

However, since *Godly Play* is primarily a Sunday school method, it is not directly suitable for the Finnish public school classroom. The most complicated issue is that religious education is non-confessional by nature. Therefore in order to use *Godly Play* in the Finnish school context the model will need to be simplified. The school version could include the presentation, the wondering questions and the children's individual responses to what they have heard and experienced. However, prayers, hymns and other kinds of religious practices would have to be left out even though pupils are supposed to be offered an opportunity to take part in traditional Christian festivals and to pass on the Christian tradition within the framework of the school's everyday activities. Therefore the use of *Godly Play* in the public schools needs further thought. Such modifications might be understood as a misuse of the method, but all basic educational elements are still included.

Godly Play is based on scripts. Berryman and others have written manuscripts for presentations including gestures, outlining the core idea of the story, and a very important part: *I wonder questions*. Typically, the story-teller poses *I wonder questions* to children and they respond. The parable is held in a golden box. When the storyteller takes, for example, velvet from the box, he or she could say: 'I wonder what this might be.' The children can answer if they want to. The most radical part is that there are no right answers. Playing with stories is also great fun because the atmosphere for the tasks arising from that moment is very open.

Curricula Objectives and Godly Play

The objectives for the first five school years accommodate the use of *Godly Play* very well. From our experience, it is a surprising method to the children that leads to the objectives almost directly. That is why it seems an important addition to the teachers' toolbox.

The first objective is that: 'The pupils will learn confidence in life and in themselves, learn to meet the future courageously, understand the sacred dimension, and see the influence of religion in their own personal lives and the lives of others'.[1]

Through *Godly Play* the pupil can develop an understanding of the sacred dimension because the story is experienced very intensively. Especially the '*I wonder*' form of questions provides great opportunities for individual thinking.

The second objective is: 'to get an introduction to the New Testament and the life and teachings of Jesus', and the third one: 'to get an introduction to the Old Testament's main narratives'.

It is obvious that *Godly Play* gives a comprehensive introduction to the Bible. If we are talking about narratives, *Godly Play* is very near to the original oral storytelling tradition through which the history of the Bible was originally transmitted. Parables and sacred stories from *Godly Play* can thus support meeting this objective.

The fourth objective is 'to understand the connection between the ecclesiastical year and the life of Jesus'. The fifth is 'to get an introduction to the Lutheran Church and to Lutheran congregational activities'. To meet this objective, liturgical stories can be used.

The relation of objective six to *Godly Play* is less obvious, as it aims to 'introduce other Christian churches and the environment of religious and nonreligious philosophies'.

On the other hand, objective seven can be clearly connected to *Godly Play*. It is to: 'Learn to ponder ethical questions, share their feelings and experiences, and apply Christian ethics'. The process of introducing the story creates a very open and welcoming atmosphere for responses. The provision of this kind of safe space helps to encourage expressing individual opinions.

It is striking that six out of seven main objectives for RE can easily be addressed through *Godly Play*. On that basis, the method appears very well suited for Finnish schools.

Syllabus content and Godly Play

The core contents of the syllabus often correspond directly to Berryman's manuscripts for the presentations (Berryman, 1995a, b, c; 2002a; b, c; 2004a, b, 2005).

Trust and security are mentioned as core contents in the syllabus. Related to these are questions of life and death arising from the pupils' experiences and life situations. God the Father and Creator, the Lord's blessing and Jesus' teachings about God's care are also mentioned in this context. The presentation of the Good shepherd from the *Godly Play* parables fits in very well here.

1 See the website of the National Board of Education www.oph.fi for information about the objectives including primary curricula in English.

'A valuable and unique life' is another of the core contents. Bible stories associated with the theme are essential. Among others, the 'Creation presentation' can be understood from this perspective.

Biblical stories and teachings are essential parts of the syllabus. Three major story complexes are mentioned: (1) the story of the beginning and of the Patriarchs, (2) the journey from Egypt to the Promised Land, (3) Jesus' life and teachings; the Lord's Prayer. All of these can be found in the existing *Godly Play* sacred stories and parables.

Promoting ethical values through education is also part of the basic *Godly Play* presentations. The value of each individual human being, especially from the perspective of creation, is explored in the 'Creation presentation'. The Ten Commandments are also the subject of one of the basic stories of the method.

Lutheran Church life, as mandated in the syllabus, includes festivals of the ecclesiastical and calendar year and their Christian meaning and customs. These are explored in the liturgical stories. For example, the 'church year clock' and Easter story are both very well suited to the *Godly Play* tool kit.

The religious world surrounding the pupils is a very important core content. It covers the religions and churches encountered by the pupils in Finland and elsewhere. This also includes the common and divergent features of Judaism, Christianity, and Islam. This area is not easily covered with the basic tools of the Finnish *Godly Play* school model.

The national board of education has worked out criteria for 'good learning' in the fifth grade. These include several goals that can be achieved through *Godly Play*. A common task is that the pupils should have knowledge of key aspect of the Bible and the Evangelical Lutheran Church of Finland, and that they should know how to use what they have learned to acquire more knowledge. In more concrete terms this means that the pupils should know the main Bible stories and that they understand religion as a phenomenon. Then they will understand the nature of religious language usage and recognise religious symbols, concepts, and metaphors. In Berrymans theory, religious language has a very important role (Berryman, 2004:I-II; 2005). In fact, the entire approach is based on it.

3. Perspectives

After determining the connection points between the curricula and *Godly Play*, the issue became more practical. Who is able to do the presentations and can lead the teaching? One solution is provided by combining two different programmes. Teachers are trained for *Godly Play*. This was begun in a cooperation between the University of Helsinki Teacher Training Department and the Institute for RE. At the University, teacher training students get a brief introduction to the method of *Godly Play*. Teachers in schools can receive *Godly Play* training at the institute. Another model is based on a *Godly Play* co-operation network.

The Godly Play Co-operation Network

Because the teacher training system is quite slow, Finnish *Godly Play* enthusiasts have developed a model for co-operation between parishes and schools. The basic idea is simple: pastors and youth workers trained in *Godly Play* visit schools, holding presentations in classrooms. Afterwards, the teacher guides the further process. This activity has already been tried in every grade at school.[2] Some examples:

The Hakunila parish has developed sacred stories for grades 7-9. The basic idea was to take a desert box to school and tell stories about Moses. Feedback from the teachers has been grateful and positive. Teaching the Old Testament is a complicated issue when you face students who have reached the age of puberty. It is particularly difficult to concentrate on a single Bible story. *Godly Play* has helped with this. After that, it is easier for teachers to follow the curriculum.

The Sipoo parish has used the model in pre-school. A storyteller visits pre-schools and gives presentations. In this case the development has been surprising. Rumours about exciting Bible stories have created a situation where all teachers and kitchen staff want to see the children listen to and interact with the visiting storyteller. Teachers continued to work with the method independently afterwards in this case.

There are many examples of this kind of co-operation. In this model *Godly Play* material is easy to get and also the storyteller is well trained. This success story has been based on church-style *Godly Play* training, but the method has been adjusted for the school. This has meant excluding prayers and similar devotional activities.

Experiments in Primary School

Sari Nevalainen from the Institute for RE has conducted some experiments in Meilahti primary school, situated in the Helsinki area. Her major interests have been the introspection process of the teacher and observations of events at school when the presentations are made.

She gave the same presentation to every grade from 1-6. Each time there were about 20 pupils in the classroom. She always structured her lessons the same way: first, a discussion about Christmas and the waiting period before the festival took place. Then she told everyone that there was going to be an adventure. After that she gave the Advent presentation from *Godly Play*.

---

2 The following part is based on unpublished reports of the Finnish Institute for RE In Service Training (UPI).

A discussion always ensued and questions about details of the Christmas story and its characters were asked.

Responses and further progress were conducted by the class teacher. Pupils were very willing to return to the story again and discuss it and teachers were invariably very interested in the material, but the most important finding was the silence during the story. Teachers valued concentration very highly. The 'problem' of non-confessional RE did not surface in this situation (UPI, 2004).

The story was exactly the same at every grade, but the level of the follow up process was different. Older children were very much interested in telling the story by themselves. Smaller children were fascinated by drawing and tactile materials (UPI, 2004).

The main result of this study was that *Godly Play* integrates well into Finnish primary school if the method is understood as a pedagogical tool for some RE-lessons. The basic method is always the same, but the resulting responses depend on the age and the group context (UPI, 2004).

References

Berryman, J. (1995a) *Godly Play: An imaginative approach to religious education* (Minneapolis, Augsburg).

Berryman, J. (1995b) *Teaching godly play: the Sunday morning handbook* (Nashville, Abingdon Press).

Berryman, J. (1995c) *The complete guide to godly play : an imaginative method for presenting scripture stories to children/ Jerome W. Berryman volume 3:20 presentations for winter* (Denver, Living the Good News).

Berryman, J. (2002a) *The complete guide to godly play: an imaginative method for presenting scripture stories to children/ Jerome W. Berryman volume 2:14 presentations for fall* (Denver, Living the Good News).

Berryman, J. (2002b) *The complete guide to godly play: an imaginative method for presenting scripture stories to children/ Jerome W. Berryman volume 1: How to lead godly play lessons* (Denver, Living the Good News).

Berryman, J. (2002c) *The complete guide to godly play : an imaginative method for presenting scripture stories to children/ Jerome W. Berryman volume 4:20 presentations for spring* (Denver, Living the Good News).

Berryman, J. (2004a) *I, Suuri leikki – ohjaajan opas* (Helsinki, Lastenkeskus).

Berryman, J. (2004b) *II, Suuri leikki – Uuden testamentin kertomuksia ja vertauksia adventista alkaen* (Helsinki, Lastenkeskus).

Berryman, J. (2005) *III Suuri Leikki – vanhan testamentin kertomuksia* (Helsinki, Lastenkeskus).

Kosunen, E. & Luodeslampi, J. (2005) *Church at Play.* http://www.evl-slk.fi/pdf/Church%20at%20play%20netti.pdf (accessed 2 February, 2007).

Luodeslampi, J. (2004) Godly Play, in: L. Heinonen, J. Luodeslampi & L. Salmensaari (Eds.) *Lapsityön käsikirja* (Helsinki, Kirjapaja).

Luodeslampi, J. & Nevalainen, S. (2005) Godly Play, in: A. Kallioniemi & J. Luodeslampi (Eds.) *Uskonnonopetus uudella vuosituhannella* (Helsinki, Kirjapaja).

Saine, H. (2000) *Uskonnonopetus Suomen oppivelvollisuuskoulussa 1900-luvulla* (Turku, Turun yliopiston julkaisuja, Sarja C, Scripta lingua Fennica edita).

UPI 2004. Unpublished archive about GP experiment.

UPI 2005. Unpublished archive about GP in Finland.

http://www.evl.fi (Lutheran Church in Finland), (accessed 29 August, 2005).
http.://www.oph.fi (National board of education), (accessed 29 August, 2005).
http://www.oph.fi/Subpage.asp?path=1,17627 (National board of education),
(accessed 29 August, 2005).
http://www.suol.fi (RE teachers association), (accessed 29 August, 2005).

Theologising with Children in Classrooms in Germany

Petra Freudenberger-Lötz and Friedhelm Kraft

Introduction

In recent years a change in perspective with regard to the image of the child can be observed in the field of educational theory, in schools and in work with children in church. It is based on the constructivist suggestion that the child constructs his/her own world view. This suggests we should put the capacity of the child at the centre of teaching and learning. Consequently a key task for education is to value and explore the specific world views of children and to learn from their ways of thinking. These pedagogical principles constitute the basis of a new approach to religious education (RE) in Germany that has been developed during the last few years under the headline *Theologising with Children*. This chapter aims to give an overview of the theory and practice of Theologising with Children in Germany.

In order to understand this new approach we must set it in its wider educational context. RE in Germany is organised in collaboration between the state and the religious communities. In accordance with the Basic Law (Grundgesetz) RE's basic outlook is confessional or denominational, integrating pedagogical and theological perspectives in the shape of RE. Similarly, Theologising with Children can be valued as a new perspective of teaching RE that takes into account pedagogical and theological issues.

1. School System, Primary School and Religious Education

In Germany legislation for and administration of the education system is primarily the responsibility of the federal states (Bundesländer). Compulsory education begins at age six. Primary education is provided at primary schools (Grundschulen) from the first to the fourth school year (in Berlin and Brandenburg to the sixth year). General lower secondary schools build on the primary education. In most Länder these are the *Hauptschule, Realschule, Gymnasium* and *Gesamtschule*. After years nine or ten students can continue either in general upper secondary education (Gymnasiale Oberstufe) or in the so-called 'dual system' providing vocational education and training or mixed general and vocational education. After the shock of the low ranking of German students in the international PISA study (Programme for International Student Assessment) the reform of the education system has been given a high political priority as governments of the Länder seek to promote new ways of organising the education system. The new aims and instruments are controversial, and agreements at national level seem far away. Key areas of the reform are the provision of greater autonomy for individual public schools and a new system of school inspection. Key areas of debate include new approaches to staff planning, financial resources and quality management, revised school scheduling, greater openness of schools to the community and civil organisations, and issues of standards, external evaluation, supervision, school inspection and consultation. In short, new approaches to the public school system seek to promote greater local autonomy whilst insisting on external accountability. These changes are taking place in the context of a wider debate about the establishment of standards in education. For the first time in the history of the German school system it is expected that the results of teaching and learning should be systematically evaluated. The focus is no longer on the material content of the curriculum, but on the measurement of educational standards and learning outcomes over specified periods of teaching in schools.

Figure 1: The German school system

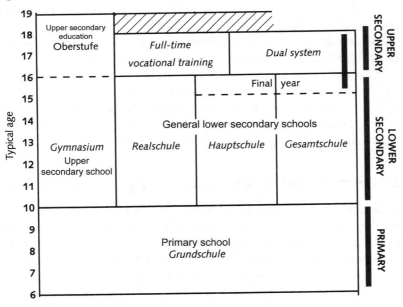

Religious Education

As we noted earlier, RE in German schools is organised through collaboration between the state and the religious communities. It is the only school subject guaranteed in the German Constitution (Grundgesetz). In Article 7, chapter 3, RE is identified as an 'ordinary school subject' that has to be taught 'in accordance with the principles of the religious communities'.[1] The state is responsible to provide the framework for religious education and the religious communities are generally responsible for learning objectives and teaching contents. RE in Germany has a confessional Christian (Protestant or Roman Catholic) basis. In some areas pilot schemes for Islamic RE are in operation, and Jewish and Orthodox Christian RE is also provided on parental demand.

Pupils have the right to opt out from RE on the grounds of freedom of religion. This must be formally declared by the parents for pupils under the age of 14, and by the pupils themselves once they reach 15. Pupils who do not participate in RE normally have to attend an alternative subject such as Ethics, Practical Philosophy, Philosophising with Children, or Values and Norms (related to each of the Bundesländer).

Since its establishment as a school subject in Germany in the 1950's, RE has been based on clear pedagogical and general educational principles; as part of the school curriculum, it provides a specific contribution to education. The Evangelical Church in Germany (EKD) has often expressed a clear vision of RE's role within the framework of the German school system. Based on the suggestion that RE should contribute to the pupils' identity formation and to develop their religious competence, the Evangelical Church has promoted personal development and religious understanding as the main aims of RE. The EKD has proposed the combination of a cluster of existing subjects, drawing together RE and various approaches to the teaching of ethics and philosophy in school (Fächergruppe). The aim is to promote mutual acceptance of different courses and provide pupils with a wider range of choices. Some states have introduced this form of cooperation; in others research is currently being conducted into dialogical models of cooperation between Roman Catholic and Protestant RE. The cluster-model supports mutual understanding between different religious and secular world views and explores ways of engaging with differences between them, thereby ensuring that such differences are neither ignored nor neglected. But we have to consider that the status of alternative secular-based ethical and philosophical courses varies across different German states.

Two main arguments can be put forward for teaching RE in distinct groups divided according to religions or denominational differences:

---

1 For historical reasons the regulations of RE in the Bundesländer of Bremen, Berlin and Brandenburg are different.

1. The authentic representation of a specific religious world view, through the transmission of basic systematic knowledge in a form likely to enhance personal insight and understanding, is likely to be more effective when undertaken in the context of separate religious instruction provided to pupils from particular religious or denominational communities;
2. Though children can learn to understand theological concepts at an early age, it is only when the necessary level of clarity is preserved through theological conversation with their peers that they can develop their own theologies and acquire a basic and coherent understanding of their religion.

Religious Education in Primary Schools

The primary school is the only type of school in Germany that must be attended by all children of school age for the first four (or six) years. In most Bundesländer, classes are only held during the morning. In reaction to social changes and their impact on children's development, a significant change has taken place in primary schools during the last ten years. With the introduction of new concepts of teaching and learning, together with the testing of new forms of school organisation, the primary school has become a driving force of reforming the whole school system.

The introduction of a regular structure (Rhythmisierung) in morning school classes and of standard half-day schooling, the integration of school entrance classes with learning groups made up of children of different ages, together with the establishment of a weekly schedule, staged learning, free structured work and project classes are all crucial factors in school development programs that have led to the creation of a number of different school profiles. However, it is fair to say that these changes have not taken place in every classroom. Many primary schools do not yet embrace an approach to education that is closely oriented to the reality of the lives of their children.

As RE is normally taught for two hours per week as a distinctive school subject in separate classes according to the denominations (Protestant/ Catholic), the question arises of how RE can contribute to this process of school development. There have been attempts to introduce common RE classes and so avoid separating pupils into different faith groups. However, the importance of religion for the development of the child's personality is acknowledged, and RE is generally seen as an essential part of general education.

The main objectives of RE can be summarised in the following way:
- Children should have the opportunity to encounter religious interpretations of the world and experience positive religious views of the world as 'life affirming';

- Children should become acquainted with the essentials of a religious tradition, and learn to understand and respect other traditions – especially those represented by their classmates.

2. Methods and Example of Good Practice

The recollection of religious traditions and 'the cultivation of cultural memory' (Jan Assmann) are major issues in RE today. Helmut Hanisch and Anton Bucher, in a study of 4th grade girls and boys from Berlin and the state of Baden-Württemberg, discovered that 'without religious classes (...) more than half of all the children would hardly be familiar with biblical stories at all' (Hanisch & Bucher, 2002:62).

Taking into account the frequently heard complaints of a demolition of religious tradition, how can religious knowledge and children's questions be related? What is the relationship between children's questions and the theological thinking of adults? Under headings such as 'Child Theology' and 'Theologising with Children', a new methodological approach has emerged in recent years designed to enable RE to deal with these questions (cp. Kraft, 2004).

Change of Perspectives (Perspektivenwechsel)

'Child Theology' and 'Theologising with Children' have developed as themes that are discussed under the heading of the 'Change of Perspectives' approach. In 1994 the synod of the Evangelische Kirche in Deutschland (EKD; Evangelical Church in Germany) sought to incorporate these themes into RE. The synod seeks 'to learn to think from a child's way of thinking', and to acknowledge and discuss 'children's own views of life and the world'. The picture of a child established in developmental psychology and social scientific research into childhood has influenced the Child Theology project. A Change of Perspectives becomes apparent in proportion to the extent in which children are viewed as subjects and actors in their own world. Childhood is explored in the light of children's views of their world and of the things they consider important: children are perceived as constructors of their own reality, as being actively involved in conceiving their world. From the perspective of RE, empirical studies dealing with the way children think are of great importance.

Child Theology and Child Philosophy

Child Theology is influenced by the Philosophising with Children movement, which has been developed in Germany since the 1990's as a result of impulses from the Anglo-Saxon world. It has had a particular impact on approaches to ethical instruction at the primary school level. Even though there are now signs that the model of cooperative RE – the cluster model – is gradually being realised in school practice, Theologising with Children undoubtedly constitutes a reaction and response to the wide-ranging debate on the subject of 'Philosophising with Children'. Just as the autonomous theological thoughts of children are acknowledged in Child Theology, Child Philosophy emphasises the importance of philosophic insights of children and confirms children's own independent philosophical competence. However clear border lines cannot be drawn between Child Philosophy and Child Theology, and despite the fact that there is a considerable level of overlap between the two, a crucial difference should be noted. The German scholar Karl Ernst Nipkow describes this difference using the question of God as an example: When speaking to children about theological issues, the question is 'who is "God" for me', but when speaking to children about philosophical matters, the question can only be 'what "God" may be' (Nipkow 1998:222).

Admittedly, this difference is all the more difficult to draw the younger the children are.

It should be kept in mind that Child Philosophy and Child Theology enjoy a common concern, namely to support and accompany children in their ability to marvel and question. In this respect, the perspective of Rainer Oberthür on the practice of RE in schools deserves closer attention: as a result of his practical work, he has developed a 'theory of religious education based on questions', in which children's specific questions constitute the starting point of his methodological reflections and teaching practices. Similar to other scholars working on 'Child Theology', Oberthür also accepts the premises raised by authors on the subject 'Philosophising with Children', and with an eye to 'Child Philosophy' he uses the term 'philosophising' in religious school education (Oberthür 1995; 1998).

The Meaning of Religious Learning

In identifying the child as a subject of learning, supporting self-guided learning processes, and taking children seriously as theologians, who construct and explain their religious world views, 'Theologising with Children' takes into account that children are in themselves active meaning-makers. This basic understanding of learning shapes the cycle of teaching and learning. This includes also taking the children's age and the subject matter into consideration. The as well needed 'transmission' aspect of education is a complementary dimension when it comes to the encounter with theological issues. Traditionally the opposite has been the case, with theological or more importantly biblical content providing the basic framework of 'Child Theology'. 'Theologising with children', or acceptance of the children's perspective, provides to a new way of handling the central questions and topics of Christian faith. The question of the 'right way' is replaced by a number of possible 'theologies of children' that pupils develop through their encounter and engagement with primarily biblical contents. They are thus able to formulate and reflect on their faith and enter into discussion with the religious ideas held by other children.

How can 'Theologising with Children' be practiced successfully?

'Theologising with children' assumes that the teachers 'have settled their relationship to their own childhood faith, religious ideas and world views, often as a result of conflict-laden detachment processes, so that they are open to children's ideas and arguments' (Schweitzer, 2003:17). In other words, the biographic confrontation with one's own childhood faith is one of the basic prerequisites for 'theologising with children'. It has also become apparent that 'child theology' requires a certain attitude on the part of the teachers – an attitude of curiosity, of wanting to know and being aware of the religious ideas and concepts that children produce as subjects of their own independent religious reflections. One of the main tasks of child-theological research will therefore lie in gaining as much empirical evidence as possible on how children of different age groups and contexts deal with theological questions and concepts. At the same time, their ability to understand and interpret biblical stories must be perceived and recognised. This must be considered the task of religious-pedagogical research, but it is also an important action-research task for teachers themselves. Petra Freudenberger-Lötz, who favours the term 'theological conversations with children' over 'child theology', looks at the importance and necessity of the further development of discussion when teaching school children. In determining the criteria for theological conversations with children, Freudenberger-Lötz deals with the question of the importance of content, the question of knowledge networking, and the recognition of children's intuitive theories (Freudenberger-Lötz, 2003:246f; 271).

In addition it should be emphasised that a connection between a 'Theology *of* Children', 'Theologising *with* Children' and a 'Theology *for* Children' has to be sought in such talks. This means that if we make an effort to perceive the theology *of* children attentively, we can recognise which questions there are in children's minds and therefore the agenda for further discussion they establish for themselves. The children's comments can form a prelude to theologising *with* children this way. The point here is to pick up the children's questions and concerns and discuss them *with* them. As a next step, their questions and concerns should be structured and developed carefully. Eventually, theology *for* children can be understood as a theology that offers children stories and models for further discussion from the Christian-Biblical tradition which they can then use for their questions and interpretation efforts.

'Child Theology' or 'theological talks with children' will determine the success of RE in primary schools by creating concrete pedagogical aids in the light of theory and practice, and by developing a 'map' to demonstrate the way children think of certain theological subjects and questions, and thereby leading the way to 'theological conversations with children'. Furthermore, it is of great importance that teachers keep learning not only how to deal with surprising comments from their pupils but also to realise *within* the speaking situation how they can pick up the children's prolific thoughts. This necessitates the establishment of a specific professional approach amongst teachers that must be introduced at the very beginning of their teacher-training.[2]

Theological conversation with children about the topic 'Angels'

Preliminary Thoughts

Both children and adults are deeply fascinated by angels. Indeed, the last years can almost talk of as a period of 'angel-boom'. Most primary students have a concrete idea of angels, imagining them with wings, halos and golden or white robes etc. Angel images can be found in our concrete living environment, are constantly present in the media, and are – of course – linked to the Christmas story.

The following example of the 4th grade of a primary school elucidate the aspects of theologising with children identified above: it shows how the specific images of the children are picked up by the teacher and, as the conversation develops, how children can indeed express their thoughts very diversely if they are inspired adequately. The example also makes clear that children can have conversations among themselves, pick up their classmates' ideas, and inspire and encourage one another. It finally shows how teachers can interact with their students and assist them in the further development of their own interpretations by relating them to the message of the Holy Bible. In short, the example demonstrates how a reasonable link between 'Theology *of* Children', 'Theologising *with* Children' and 'Theology *for* Children' can be made.

Step I: Express one's own ideas and make them part of the conversation

In the following sequence of a religious class the children get their impulse to present their own images about angels from working with psalms and

---

2 Petra Freudenberger-Lötz' current project with students of the University of Education of Karlsruhe is the 'Research Workshop Theological Talks with Children'. The core of this project is that the University students choose a way that gradually enhances the complexity of theological talks when talking theologically with children. First experiences show substantial progress in conversational skills of the involved University students (cp. Freudenberger-Lötz 2004).

relating them to their own lives. During a discussion in class the majority of the children chose psalm 91, verse 11 as their favourite psalm: 'For He shall give His angels charge over you, to keep you in all your ways'. In the first part of the following conversation the students explain how they imagine angels.

Alessio	With wings and here a circle, a golden one (points at a halo above his head), that shines.
Klaus	The wings are white. Angels have a white robe and bring God messages. Because, maybe God can't see everything and then angels look for him around and maybe they write down what they see on scrolls and then they give them to God.
Verena	I imagine angels with wings and adorned with gold.
Lena	I imagine angels white with yellow wings and a halo.
Tim	I don't believe that angels have wings, and I also don't really think that they have a halo. I rather believe that they are messengers and look like us, but just give messages, like Klaus said. They deliver messages, but look ordinary.
Teacher	Do they look like normal people? Does that mean that you can see angels?
Milena	I don't think that you can see Angels. But if it was right what Tim said, it might be possible to see angels then. But I don't really think so.
Tim	I can imagine angels to be visible very well. We can't see the angels themselves, but if an angel places itself into somebody, so that this person partly is the angel, this way we can see it partly.
Teacher	So do you mean that angels go into a person and this person delivers messages then? [Tim nods heavily]. Aha. (Alessio calls 'Ah')
Alessio	I once attended church, and there the priest said that God or an angel can go into my mother and my mother can forgive me then, although it was God or an angel, who was inside my mother.
Verena	Sometimes you also say to someone else: 'You're an angel'. Maybe sometimes angels go into us and then we are nice.

When taking a closer look at this sequence, it becomes apparent that the children's images of angels first concentrate on what angels could look like. In doing so the children have some specific and traditional images of angels (white, golden, wings, halos). Klaus expands this image by placing emphasis on the role that angels have: being the messengers and servants of God, 'helping' God to solve the problem of ubiquity. As a result, Tim picks up Klaus' thought, but then comes up with a new and surprising thesis to be discussed: angels have no wings and no halo but look 'like us'. As the teacher shows interest in his idea, Tim modifies his image a bit: angels themselves don't look like human beings but they can go into them and make them messengers of God. They make this person carry God's love and kindness into the world. Alessio points out by his comment that he thinks that there is a strong connection between God and angels. God acts in human beings through angels. The conversation doesn't end at this point, though the details of what is said cannot be provided here due to lack of space. For example, the children talk later about the images that they have of guardian angels and also refer to the question of theodicy this way. This makes Tim raise some interesting aspects, which his classmates pick up, and want to know more about and which they relate to their own thoughts.

In a second sequence of the conversation, the teacher asks the children what makes them imagine angels with wings and halos and what meaning these attributes have for them. The children report that they have seen such images of angels many times before and that they have adopted this image because it shows the meaning of angels for people.

Milena	When I think of a halo I always believe that the angel is sacred, and when I know that, I don't need to be afraid.
Klaus	To me being sacred also means that they are precious. Angels are precious and dear to me.
Alessio	The wings show us that angels can be inside us and then can go to God to deliver a message to him.
Tim	I think that silver, gold and other precious colours are supposed to represent the grand and precious angel.

While presenting specific but diverse images in the first sequence of the conversation, the children now expand these images by trying to fathom and reflect the symbolism of the attributes. Interestingly enough, the specific and symbolic meaning can stand parallel without any problem. Neither the children see a contradiction in this nor does the teacher demand a decision from the students by making them choose only one meaning. At this point of the conversation, children can and are allowed to have different point of views, the only thing they are being requested to do is to justify their point of views. Thus Klaus and Tim justify their opinions, whether angels have wings, as follows:

Klaus	Angels have less power than God, that's why they need wings. God doesn't need any wings.
Tim	Angels are divine. Everything that is divine can go to heaven. It doesn't need any wings.

All in all, the teacher fulfils an important role in theological discussion: he or she should take the students' ideas seriously by picking them up and making them part of the conversation. When children expand their images in the course of the talk, the teacher should carefully inspire the children, but never demote their concrete images as insufficient. If these guidelines are realised during class, the teacher can succeed in inspiring the children to engage with diverse theological images – these are an important basis for successful religious development.[3]

In summary it can be said that this first step in teaching places emphasis on a 'Theology of Children' and on 'Theologising with Children'. What is required next is a 'Theology for Children', that is to offer children models for further discussion, pictures and stories, that also includes possible answers to controversial questions of the children. In addition, they should inspire children to broaden their knowledge and images of angels. This process takes place in the following second step of the teaching.

Step II: Dealing with children's questions

As a second step of instruction, some of the children's central questions about angels, which came up during the first step, are now picked up. Each student is supposed to choose one of the questions that are personally most significant to him or her. Next, they get a 'research assignment': this takes place in a complex and inspiring learning environment. The children are now asked to write down their own answers to the chosen questions and/or to visualise their answers in a picture. After this they start to explore the biblical verses and stories that have been set up for them by the teacher. The students seek new inspirations to expand the image they started from. In addition, the teacher offers the children stories and conversations as well as structuring support. The students write down their new insights. Finally, they exchange their learning experiences and results with their classmates.[4] Whereas the first step of instruction was held predominantly orally, the children's previous images and learning results are now put into writing and drawing. The diversity found in the final compositions of the children clearly demonstrates the positive output of such religious instructions.

---

3 Reto Fetz has shown in an empirical study that a continuous religious development (contrary to the much-cited 'break' during adolescence) is more likely to succeed, if a diverse inspiration to reflect and to enhance own images takes place during infancy (cp. Fetz, 1995).

4 All in all this instruction is constructivist-oriented: it begins with individual images of the students and offers an inspiring learning environment, in which previous images can be developed independently and own learning experiences can become transparent (cp. Gerstenmaier & Mandl, 1995).

Research Task 3:

Do angels go into a person or are they companions all along?
Are both options possible?

1. In the beginning I thought:
   That angels could not slip into human beings.

2. In the Bible I can find answers for this question.
   I have found the following Biblical sayings:

   a) 'For he will command his angels concerning you to guard in all your ways.
      On their hands they will bear you up, so that you will not dash you foot
      against a stone.' (Ps 91:11-12)

   b) It will happen: next year this time Sara will have a baby. Abraham thought:
      this foreigner is the Lord. He is coming to me in the figure of a human being.
      And his companions are angels. Then the three men set out from there.

3. Why are these biblical sayings answers for the question of research?

Saying a)	Saying b)
The angels are taking care of human beings.	*He can slip into a human being.*

4. This is how I answer the research question in my own way:
   They can slip into human beings and they protect them.

Learning options

The example shows a successful connection between a 'Theology *of* Children' (to express imaginations) and 'Theologising *with* Children' (to develop ideas by talking). Moreover the children have got the opportunity to acquire knowledge and answers to open issues: that means a 'Theology *for* children' (biblical verses and stories, which deliver answers; specific hints and tasks). The project shows a constructive perspective of teaching and learning as a feature of 'Theologising with Children'. And the example shows only a part of the whole teaching project.

3. Perspectives

'Child Theology' has been established as a new perspective and model in the field of RE. Whereas at an early stage only children were mentioned as 'theologians', now also 'Theologising with Youth' has appeared as a new theme within the debate of 'Theologising'. An outstanding is how best to train teachers to practice 'theological conversation' with children and students.

From a methodological perspective we can categorise 'Theologising' in three ways:
- − 'Theologising' as an acquisition of a religious competence;
- − 'Theologising' as a suitable form of confrontation with religion within schools;
- − 'Theologising' as a bridge to other forms and places of 'living' religions.

'Theologising' gives a specific contribution to acquire religious competence. Religious competence here is defined as an integrated disposal referring to knowledge, understanding, attitude and the ability to value and act.

The methodological approach to 'Theologising' enables RE to function as a specific form of engagement with religion, without compromising the principles of 'learning' and 'acquisition', or the perspective of teachers and learners.

'Theologising' emphasises the structure of RE as a subject of teaching and learning. Religion as a living phenomenon and a practical 'doing' (rituals, feasts etc.) is not underestimated. On the contrary: 'Theologising' leads children and students to religion as a living practice: thus religion constitutes an important dimension of the culture of schools and school program.

References

Büttner, G. (2002) *Jesus hilft! Untersuchungen zur Christologie von Schülerinnen und Schülern* [*Jesus helps. Studies on Concepts of Christ by Students*] (Stuttgart).

Fetz, R. (1995) Der Kinderglaube. Seine Eigenart und seine Bedeutung für die spätere Entwicklung [The Faith of the Child. Its character and influence on further development], in: E. Groß (Ed.) *Der Kinderglaube. Perspektiven aus der Forschung für die Praxis [The Faith of the Child. Perspectives from research for practice]* (Donauwörth).

Freudenberger-Lötz, P. (2003) *Religiöse Bildung in der Schuleingangsstufe. Religionspädagogische und grundschulpädagogische Perspektiven [Religious Education in the school reception stage. Perspectives of religious education and primary school]* (Stuttgart).

Freudenberger-Lötz, P. (2004) *Einblicke in die 'Forschungswerkstatt theologische Gespräche mit Kindern' [Insights in the 'Research workshop on theological talks with children']* (Karlsruhe).

Gerstenmaier, J. & Mandl, H. (1995) Wissenserwerb unter konstruktivistischer Perspektive [Knowledge acquirement in a constructivist perspective], *Zeitschrift für Pädagogik,* 41 (6), 867-888.

Härle, W. (2004) Was haben Kinder in der Theologie verloren? Systematisch-theologische Überlegungen zum Projekt einer Kindertheologie [What business do children have in theology? Systematic-theological thoughts for a project of children's theology], in: *Jahrbuch für Kindertheologie* Bd. 3 (Stuttgart).

Hanisch, H. & Bucher, A. (2002): *Da waren die Netze randvoll. Was Kinder von der Bibel wissen [Then the nets were completely filled up. What children know from the Bible]* (Göttingen).

Kraft, F. (2004) 'Theologisieren mit Kindern' – ein neues didaktisches Leitbild für den Religionsunterricht der Grundschule?" [Theologising with Children. A new guiding method for Religious Education in primary school], *theologische beiträge,* 35 (2), 81-91.

Nipkow, K. E. (1998) *Bildung in einer pluralen Welt [Education in a plural world]* Bd. 2: Religionspädagogik im Pluralismus (Gütersloh).

Oberthür, R. (1995) *Kinder und die großen Fragen [Children and the big questions]* Ein Praxisbuch für den Religionsunterricht (München).

Oberthür, R. (1998) *Kinder fragen nach Leid und Gott. Lernen mit der Bibel im Religionsunterricht [Children ask about suffering and about God. Learning with the Bible in Religious Education]* (München).

Schweitzer, F. (2003) Was ist und wozu Kindertheologie? [What and what for Children's theology?], in: *Jahrbuch für Kindertheologie* Bd.2 (Stuttgart).

Teaching Religion through Art in Religious Education in Italian Schools

Maria Luisa Mazzarello

Introduction

This article presents the situation in Italy concerning the teaching of religion in schools with particular emphasis on Roman Catholicism. The Italian model can only be understood in the light of the history of the relationship between Church and State and the school-society dynamic.

The article will give a panoramic view of the place of religion in the primary school without dwelling on the details of the Italian context. Within the framework of the recent school reform, religion is now establishing its position in school and its place among the other subjects in the school curriculum.

The second part of the article will present an example of good practice in RE. In Italy, various models and teaching methods are used in the teaching of RE in schools. In practice teaching is inspired by child centred methodologies. The teacher is committed to drawing out the motive to learn from each pupil. The pupil asks questions that require reflection and seeks responses. The textbook offers stimuli and contributes towards the reflection. The real values are the lived experiences. The goal is reflecting on personal experience in order to know and learn. The teaching method provides for interdisciplinary activities where religion occupies its own proper place.

The most meaningful methods for good practice are those that use induction, activity and research, and that start with the analysis and interpretation of documents, in particular biblical texts and Christian art.

No method can be considered as complete without running the risk of partiality in the breadth experiencing of religious culture and producing routine and monotony in the classroom. Given this awareness, the choice of method proposed here is *Teaching Religion through Art*. There are at least three reasons for this choice. The first comes from the awareness that in Italy art is being recognised as a text of the Christian tradition and therefore cannot be ignored as part of the expression of faith by a people whose cultural roots are Christian. The second reason is the attention given by the school to the local situation and its cultural expressions. The third reason comes from the awareness of the formative value of art. This is not just because we live in an era of images, but also because communicating the essential content of the Christian religion through the use of its rich artistic inheritance, in which Italy and Europe occupies a privileged place, is a wonderful opportunity for a new dialogue between religion and culture. At the same time, it is a teaching strategy that is suited to children, who learn more easily using visual methods. For all these reasons *Teaching Religion through Art* is an increasingly used method in school.

1. School system, Primary School and Religious Education

In Italy the primary school is divided into a first year (6-7 years) and two two-year periods (8-11 years). It forms part of the whole education system, which is structured as follows:

Figure 1: The Italian school system

Infant school	3 years (children from 3 to 6 years)
First cycle	
Primary School	5 years (children from 6 to 11 years)
Secondary school level one	3 years (children from 11 to 13 years)
Second cycle It is possible to choose between two courses of studies	
Lyceum	5 years (young people from 13 to 18 years). Options from the following specialisations: arts, classics, human sciences, business, languages, music, science, or technology.
Professional training and formation	variable duration, but at least 3 years. A first qualification, after three years, recognised for entry into the labour market. After 4 years it is possible to do a supplementary year and enter university.

We focus here on the primary school. Within this system, which aims to provide a broad education, the RE teacher brings his or her specific contribution to integral education of children from 6 to 11 years old. They aim to help develop the religious dimension of the pupils, committing themselves to encourage reflection on their heritage and experience and to contribute by providing a specific response to each pupil's inherent need for discovering a purpose in life.

Relationship between State, School and Religions

The national education system of Italy consists of state schools, private schools, officially recognised by the state, and schools organised by municipal agencies (under art.1.1, law n. 62/2000). The large majority of private schools are Catholic.

In 2002/2003, state schools educated 88% of the student population, and private schools, recognised by the state, were responsible for 12% (Ministero dell'Istruzione, 2004).

The teaching of religion in the state schools is based on the Catholic religion. This was established by a concordat between the Italian State and the Holy See and by successive statements of intend. Religion is part of the curriculum and has the same status as other school subjects. It is open to all pupils because of its cultural and formative value. It has been left optional only because it touches the delicate area of personal conscience.

Since 1984 the Italian State has established *binding agreements* with other recognised minority religious groups in Italy, among them, the Churches represented by the Tavola Valdese (Law 11-8-1984, n. 449); the Italian Union of Christian Churches and Seventh-day Adventists (Law 22-11-1988, n. 516); the Assemblies of God in Italy (Law 22-11-1988, n. 517); the Union of Italian Jewish Communities (Law 8-3-1989, n. 101); the Christian Union of Evangelical Baptists of Italy (Law 12-4-1995, n. 116) and the Lutheran Church (Law 29-11-1995, n. 520).

New *agreements* are being worked out with the Orthodox Church in Italy, the Italian Hindu Union, the Christian Congregation of Jehovah Witnesses and the Italian Buddhist Union.

In these *agreements* with the different religious confessions the state agrees that the state schools, within the exercise of their autonomy, will provide supplementary instruction in response to requests from the representatives of other religious groups (Ghiachi, 1989; Gianni, 1991; Lucciconi, 2003).

It is surprising to see the large number of parents of primary school children who specifically choose Christian (Catholic) Religious Education (CRE) each year. In the school year 2004/2005, 95.5% of children studied of CRE including those of non-Christian and non-practising families.

This fact could be taken as proof of the cultural value given to such teaching, whose confessional nature is fully compatible with the secular nature of the state.

The choice of confessional CRE is not tied to the faith of the pupils, but rather to the significance of the content taught. This is indispensable for a full knowledge and understanding of Italian history and culture. All this helps people to live with others with greater awareness and to share their sense of social belonging.

This specifically Italian phenomenon can be explained by historical, social and juridical factors.

CRE according to official documents

The reasons for the legitimacy of CRE in the Italian state schools derive from a series of official directives. These combine mutual respect for the perspectives of the state and of the Church. CRE therefore has some peculiarities.

It is *confessional teaching* since its content comes prevalently from the sources and history of the Christian-catholic confession. This teaching continues to show its capacity for great openness and dialogue because it develops content in an interdisciplinary manner, comparing Catholic teaching with different contemporary cultures and with other religious confessions. In this way CRE meets the needs of a changing Italian society that is becoming increasingly multi-ethnic and multi-faith.

It is a subject that shares the goals of the school, offering its own specific contribution. It makes use of a cultural approach to the theme of religion and is included into the school as a subject, with its programmes defined in the *agreement* between the Ministry for Education and the Conferenza Episcopale Italiana (CEI; Catholic Bishop's Conference of Italy).

Out of this format comes the distinction and the complementarities between teaching religion in school and the catechesis of the ecclesial community. This distinction, which has not been reached without a struggle, is now clearly stated.

The result is that, while catechesis requires a deep spiritual acceptance and aims to nourish the faith already passed on by the family or religious groups, CRE is open to all: believers, non-believers or those who belong to other faith traditions, because it does not require faith commitment. Its role is to understand a culture, to integrate with other disciplines, and to mature in respect and dialogue with other faiths and systems of meaning. By integrating with other disciplines it strengthens, develops and completes the educational task of the school and, by means of comparison, leads the young person to appreciate what is positive in those values held by other views of life, whether they are religious or secular.

It is a teaching that respects the freedom of conscience of the pupils. For this reason it can be open to all, even non-believers, requiring the professional duty of the teacher to avoid indoctrination or even simply of a catechetical form of teaching. Because this teaching is offered to all who choose it, it is subject to the choice of the parents, who will be able to opt for an alternative activity, also neither its content or its level of obligation is clearly defined at present.

The teaching is allotted two hours a week in the school timetable and uses textbooks. The texts are subject to the *nihil obstat* of the CEI, which approves them if they observe the four requirements that characterise the subject. These are: responding to the content expressed in the national standards; using teaching methods that are adequate to the age of the students; paying attention to comparison and dialogue with other faiths; paying attention to and encouraging dialogue with the other school subjects.

It is a teaching given by 'specialist' teachers, recognised as being suitable by church authorities and nominated by the school authorities, who pay them. It can also be given by 'class teachers', who declare themselves ready for such teaching and are recognised as being suitable by the church authorities.

At present, based on the Law 186/2003 for the appointment of religion teachers in state schools, as it was declared in the *agreement* of 1985, the juridical status of specialist religion teachers is recognised. This recognition, while helping to define CRE as an organic part of the school curriculum, reinforces the place of teaching religion.

For teachers, there are specific opportunities for formation in the Theological and Catechetical Faculties or Senior Colleges of Religious Sciences. These academic institutions offer a broad range of subjects, not just theology but also law, sociology, psychology, education and teaching methods. These higher education courses, which are recognised by state law, offer a complete preparation for future teachers, who not only require a complete professional training but also spiritual preparation, as well as strong motivation and ideals.

Religious Education in Primary School

Shared goals: A review of recent years identifies some relevant data regarding CRE within the school reform. An important step has been taken when we consider the fact that the state school recognises the specific contribution of CRE to the fulfilment of its goals. In fact, CRE, by valuing the principles of autonomy and personalisation:
  - favours the growth and valuing of the human person, completing his/ her formation from the religious point of view;
  - proposes teaching programmes organised according to the principle of progressive cycles that respect the rhythm of growth;
  - values the identity of each pupil, taking account of differences in religion, with a teaching method that is open to meeting and dialogue;
  - favours co-operation between school and family, recognising the knowledge of the historic, cultural and human development offered by CRE as an enrichment for the formation of the young person;
  - includes CRE into the educational plan of each school.

Integrated into the curriculum in this way, religion establishes its right to be considered a school subject with a contribution to make to education even more clearly. However, if, on the one hand we recognise its growth in quality, especially from the cultural and pedagogical point of view, on the other hand there still remains the difficulty of providing an 'alternative hour' for the children, who do not take advantage of this teaching. In this case the elements of religious culture present in the different subjects must be stressed. In Italy it seems impossible to avoid the religious dimension since culture has been permeated by Christianity for centuries as one can see from the numerous expressions of faith, especially in art.

The Syllabus: Religion, like any other subject, refers to *Specific Learning Objectives,* which are national standards that the state ensures for all pupils. Every school refers to them, ensuring the essential elements of Christianity, while respecting the culture of the school and the development of critical ability.

The *Specific Objectives* guarantee four areas of 'knowledge' and 'skills' ability.

Knowledge:
- the historical-revealed dimension expressed in Christianity: God and the human person, Jesus Christ, the Church and the moral life of the Christian;
- the sources of Christianity, with special attention to the Bible and to Christian life throughout history (tradition);
- openness to interaction with other subjects;
- 'respect' for and 'dialogue' with other faiths.

Skills:
- 'discovering skills', the ability to discover and understand signs;
- 'knowing and interpreting skills', the ability to gain knowledge, understand meanings and make links;
- 'expressing skills', the ability to use a symbolic language, to explain, to reconstruct, to develop and to supply documentary evidence;
- 'methodological skills', the ability to use research methods to gain information;
- 'evaluation skills', the ability to make critical comparisons.

The formulation of the present Christian programme in the *Specific Learning Objectives* is relevant at a primary school level both in the area of 'knowledge' and of 'skills'. Many educators recognise the contribution of CRE to the overall educational plan of the primary school because of its ethical contribution to civil life and its cultural enrichment, not only for the development of society (the cultural roots of a people), but even more for the personal development of identity.

Education for dialogue with other Churches and Christian communities and with other religions is rooted in personal and social identity. A dialogue is open to discovering shared values, such as respect for creation and for human life, awareness that God is Creator and Father and that we are all called to promote justice and peace and to safeguard the environment.

From theory to practice

The frame of reference so far outlined offers an image of the CRE where the various factors allow its complexity and difficulty to emerge as well as its significance. Realistically, the question that now arises is how this teaching works out in practice in schools.

The data gathered in the *Two-year National Experiment*, which took place in the years 1998-2000, allow us to evaluate how the teachers in the experiment kept the national standards in mind and were inspired by shared methodological criteria in their teaching (Conferenza Episcopale Italiana, 2001). They are:
- valuing the personal, social and cultural experience of the pupil;
- the progressive use of the documents of revelation;
- a meaningful approach to the language of signs and symbols that are proper to the Christian-catholic religious culture;
- meeting the witnesses of history and of today who embody religious values in a significant way;
- knowledge and appreciation of the values present in other religious traditions.

2. Methods and example of good practice

Working with art in school

Introducing pupils to the understanding of the symbols and signs of Christian art means developing their sense of beauty and transforming their approach to their artistic heritage into an aesthetic and cognitive experience of the content of the Christian credo.

Using art in teaching religion in school is an opportunity for the teacher to enrich his/her teaching with the language of images, which needs the correct hermeneutics in order to interpret the images. It is also a privileged opportunity to encourage interdisciplinary links that can involve teachers of other subjects. In this way it is easier to help the pupils to understand how every artistic production is the fruit of the culture of its time, of a way of looking at the Christian religion at a given moment in history.

The choice of a work of art, as a generator of knowledge, is based on certain convictions that guide one's teaching. If a written document expresses itself through concepts and proceeds by respecting the narrative categories of space and time, Christian art expresses itself in a very unique way:
- it is found within the order of symbols;
- it re-tells the content of the Christian sources in a visual manner;
- it offers them the tradition in terms of beauty;
- it narrates by bringing together in the same scene, events, places and times that may be far apart in reality;
- it allows the Credo of the first Christian communities to have significance in the present;
- it enables an historical-cultural inheritance to be rediscovered;
- it is a place of 'remembrance' in which Christian identity takes root.

One element that should not be ignored is choosing artistic works of different complexity according to the age and the ability of the children, remembering that every sign or expression of Christian art is a text that can be read, understood and interpreted at various levels (Tricarico, 2005).

This was the starting point for a field study undertaken in a variety of schools in Rome and its surroundings. The first experience of this action research took place from 1997-2000 and others are in progress (Pellerey, 1980). They demonstrate the interest that exists in visual teaching methods. As the research work progressed, it became clear, that using art was meaningful on two fronts: it facilitates the passing on of elements of religious content that are sometimes difficult to communicate through concepts, and it communicates religious meaning to children in a symbolic way. This helps to lead the children to arrive more easily at a correct interpretation of Christian beliefs.

Case study: the Mosaic 'God Creating Man'

Among the many research projects undertaken by teachers, we present the one undertaken with the fourth class, elementary (9-10 year-olds). The choice of this project allows us to consider the elements of the teaching method, which in turn allows us to indicate, step by step the work done in the classroom.

Requirements: It is worth noting that the pupils had already worked with works of art in other subjects. Additionally, with the assistance of the art teacher, the pupils were helped to acquire the tools needed to decode a visual text in three steps: The first step was a 'global' view, in which the approach was mainly emotional. The pupils grasped what the text was communicating with both eyes and heart. They were attracted by certain details and missed others. The second step was 'analytic', aimed at grasping all the elements of the art-text, analysing their obvious and their more symbolic meaning and discovering the relationships between them. The third step was 'synthetic'. Here the image is re-composed in its total meaning. The global message was explained and enriched by the symbolic meaning of the details.

In this way the children recognised that a picture has a structure and characteristics that need to be read and interpreted correctly.

Choosing the work of Art: The work chosen was the mosaic *God Creating Man* from the Cappella Palatina, Palermo (XII century).

There were two reasons for this choice: the work was capable of giving a religious-Christian answer to the quest for meaning: 'Where does life come from?' It is suited to children because it is important both in its elements and composition, easy to read and understand.

The choice of the picture was followed by work with the class:
- the presentation and reading of the mosaic (place, time, technique, the pupils' spontaneous reading);
- an analysis of the work of art: the objective and symbolic value of its elements (conversation);
- verbalising the message.

The approach to the work of art: Each pupil had a copy of the image to look at and analyse. The pupils already knew the technique of creating a mosaic.

To encourage the pupils to look attentively at all the elements in the mosaic, some questions were asked:
- How many areas could the picture be sub-divided into?
- What do you see in each area?
- Which are the most important elements?
- Observe and describe: the characters (position, dress, gestures, relatioships between characters, etc.) and other elements (position, form, colours).

– Do you recognise who is being portrayed in this work of art?
– Who are the characters?
– What is the overall meaning of the picture?
– What is its message?

The essential elements of the meaning of the mosaic emerged immediately from the written responses of the children. They were struck by the breath of life and the similarity between God and man. In the conversation that followed, the pupils were encouraged to engage with the symbolic elements of the picture too.

In relation to *God*:
– the halo: symbol of God's holiness;
– the face: is that usually attributed to Jesus in art, Christ the Pantocrator (Christ who reveals the Father) ;
– the breath: symbol of the Spirit who gives life;
– the scroll: symbol of wisdom;
– the hand blessing in the Byzantine way;
– the footwear, a sign of regal dignity;
– the purple coloured robe and blue mantle (divinity and humanity).

In relation to *man*:
– the face in the image of God;
– the man seated on a rock as if on a throne.

In relation to the *faces:*
– God the Father represented with the features of Jesus.
– Man represented with the features of God the Creator.

In relation to the *landscape*:
– the mountains in the background and, in the middle distance, God is bigger that the mountains, to show his power.

These are some of the comments from the children:
'God created Adam like himself; he gave him life by means of a breath. This breath makes it clear that life is a gift from God to man.' 'Adam is naked and is seated on a rock if it were a throne, because from that day he would be the lord of the earth.' 'God, with the breath of life, gave Adam intelligence and love, for this reason Adam is closer to God.' 'Some animals seem suspended in the air, others walk in a field of flowers and are going towards God and towards man. They are all in pairs.' 'There are many flowers that represent serenity.'

From these reports it can be seen that the children are capable of reading a work of art correctly and of understanding the message it gives.

Comparison with Genesis 1

The children were already familiar with the biblical text of the creation from previous years. They already had a level of understanding and it was therefore possible to proceed more quickly to the analysis of the principal components of the art-text.

At this point a deeper encounter with the biblical text was needed. It was necessary to grasp the similarities and differences between the written and the visual text, to see how the artist, with his specific sensitivity, had interpreted what was written in the Bible.

Even though not all the children were able to grasp the complementarities and mutual enrichment of the two forms of communication, the teacher was able to draw the following conclusions from their responses:

> The analysis of the work of art mediated the message of creation in an incisive way, showing the breath of the Creator God; the likeness of man to God; the position of man, naked but lord of the universe, towards whom creation converges. What was even more important was that, in responding to the questions of the children regarding God being represented with the features of His Son, from whose mouth comes the breath of life (Holy Spirit), an opportunity was provided to show how the artist expressed the faith of the Church in the creative work of the Trinity.

It is represented here by the face of Christ the Pantocrator, whose features make the Father visible and through the breath, a symbol of the spirit, the Holy Spirit. The children could only reach this theological level with the help of the art-text.

Evaluating children's learning

The mosaic of Creation aroused a greater interest in the children than was expected. They were motivated to search for other works of art dealing with creation and brought them to school.

As a result the reading and analysis of other creation scenes was chosen as a method of evaluating the work. In this way it was possible to evaluate their ability to read new images, link them with the related biblical texts and discover their underlying message.

The children were divided into groups and given pictures from the Cathedral of Montreale, each re-presenting a different scene from Genesis 1: the separation of the earth from the waters, the creation of the animals, God shows Eve to Adam, God rests.

They were similar mosaics to that of the Cappella Palatina, but with some variations. The pupils, where necessary, asked for explanations.

The result of the evaluation was satisfactory: it showed that the children had acquired the basic criteria for reading a work of Christian art. They had understood that every detail, every colour, suggests something that points beyond the appearance, to a deeper reality; they were able to recognise the biblical text that had inspired the artist.

From some elements of evaluation we note a high level of satisfaction both on the part of the teachers and of the pupils. Both groups comment on participation in research and say, 'class work is extremely motivating'. In particular, when evaluating work with Christian art, the children have used words like:

> The picture helps me to understand better... you understand immediately... It gives the idea... It represents... It reports the scene in colour... It is easier to remember, it brings it to life. You have to read the written text, it tells the minimum, it makes you imagine, but not as much ....

Realistically, it must be said that in the preparation of this method teachers found themselves faced with totally new work, which required gradual mastery, working as a team during formative sessions. One teacher put it like this:

> Class work with an art-document can seem complex, but in reality it is not if you have clear objectives to reach and if you know and use an adequate method. It is a method that requires an option for formative quality rather that quantity of content, the building of competence in place of the mechanical acquisition of concepts.

3. Perspectives

In conclusion, from the experience undertaken in a number of classes, it is clear that the method of *Teaching Religion through Art* can be characterised as *Pedagogy of Discovery* (Mazzarello & Triario, 2002-2005). It is a process that leads to the discovery of Italy's Christian artistic inheritance and that of other countries, which mediates an inculturated Gospel message.

This method requires that, at each stage, the content that one wants to get the pupils to learn in the different school classes, is identified in artworks with a view to acquiring adequate competence.

It is obvious that the artistic dimension of religious culture offers the possibility of opening links with other fields of knowledge, for example those of language and expression, and of history, geography and social studies. This very exploration leads to the knowledge of the artist and his times, as well as the place and socio-cultural context in which his artistic 'creation' first came to light. The children, observing and contemplating, listen to the work of art, which speaks to them by narrating the events of the history of salvation. Thus they get to know the Christian Credo, which though expressed in a variety of styles, always holds the same perennial message of Revelation.

Starting from the new situations that result from the school reform and from cultural changes that are constantly moving towards globalisation and religious pluralism, we note some significant aspects for the future of the teaching of religion in Italy.

These aspects refer to the very shape of religious teaching and the solution to certain problematic areas.

At present, CRE presents many valid aspects, which should be preserved and enriched in the context of the new institutional structures established by the school reform. However there are also aspects that need to be improved:

- CRE is constantly subject to 'choice' on the part of the family at the beginning of each school cycle and, thus, risks finding itself the victim of subjective choices.
- Although well defined in its curricular form it has a weak identity because of lack of clarity in evaluation. For this reason it risks being undervalued in its formative role if it this not recognised by the teaching team.
- Faced with a school system that tends to organise itself around competencies that go beyond the confines of subjects, CRE is being asked to value points of contact with other subjects. How could RE integrate fully into the primary culture and teach real competences for the pupils without losing its identity as a subject?
- Ever increasing immigration into Italy requires that account be taken of the intercultural situation and therefore of those children who attend school and who do not have Christian roots. This puts the question in a new way: how can RE help children in the process of integrating into the culture of the hosting country?

Teaching Religion through Art is a very committed method. It requires high professional quality from the teachers and good quality of text books and materials.

In order to improve their professional quality teachers need increasingly specific competences in the areas of culture and teaching methods as well as in the development of human relationships.

The authors of textbooks are constantly being encouraged to respect the specific content of CRE together with good methodological practice. To all this we must add the need for practical experimentation, with a view to formulating methods that are responsive to the needs of meaningful learning. This objective is part of the overall context of the curriculum for the Italian school.

References

Conferenza Episcopale Italiana (2001) Documento della sperimentazione nazionale sull'IRC per la formazione dei docenti di religione, *Quaderni della Segreteria della CEI*, 5 (16).

Ghiachi, G. (1989) Scuola e religione – quattro leggi a confronto, *Regno-attualità*, 18, 537-539.

Gianni, A. (1991) *L'istruzione religiosa nelle scuole italiane. La nuova normativa secondo gli accordi tra stato e confessioni religiose* (Cinisello Balsamo (MI), Edizioni Paoline), 65-69; 171-212.

Mazzarello, M.L./Rezzghie, R. (2000) Risultati della sperimentazione. Prima valutazione dei dati raccolti dai questionari, *Notiziario CEI* 4 (32), 33-36; 37-59.

Mazzarello, M.L/Triario, M.F. (2000-2005) Il mistero dell'Incarnazione 1 – La missione di Gesù 2 – Il mistero della Pasqua 3 – La chiesa nel tempo. La narrazione dell'architettura sacra 4 – La creazione 5 (Torino, Leumann; Elledici, Il Capitello).

Ministero dell'Istruzione, dell'Università & della Ricerca (2004) *Report to the Parliament on the implementation of the law 10 marzo 2000*, No. 62 (Roma).

Lucciconi, I. (2003) I rapporti tra lo Stato e le confessioni religiose 'diverse dalla cattolica', in: AA.VV., *Commentario al codice della scuola* (Brescia, La Scuola), 714-719.

Pellerey, M. (1980) Il metodo della ricerca-azione di K. Lewin nei suoi più recenti sviluppi e applicazioni, *Orientamenti Pedagogici* 27 (3), 449-463.

Specific objectives of catholic religion (2004), *DPR* 122, 30-3-2004.

Tricarico, M.F. (2005) La dimensione religiosa dell'arte contemporanea, *Religione e Scuola*, 33, (3), 65-74.

The picture on page 109 was provided by the author. It shows the mosaic 'God Creating Man' from the Cappella Palatina in Palermo/Italy.

A Focus on the Educational Quality of the Learning Process in Religious Education in the Netherlands

Henk Kuindersma and Johan Valstar

Introduction

It is eight thirty in the morning. A day at a Protestant primary school nearly always starts with the same ritual. The children and their teachers talk about current events and personal experience. Thoughts are exchanged on major events and everyday occurrences at home, in the playground and in the world. This encounter nearly always turns into a short 'celebration' with moments of learning. It involves telling stories, especially from the Bible. Depending on the objective, children philosophise about vital questions affecting their lives. These questions are often raised in response to the story. Prayer and songs are the most common forms of expression.

This article, with its basis in *mainstream* Protestant primary education, is dedicated to the examination of aspects of 'good practice' in religious education.

In section 1, there is a brief description of the context: the Dutch educational system and 'open' Protestant-Christian education.

Section 2 contains a short outline of the three most prevalent teaching methods used for religious education in the Netherlands. It examines a dual reference framework. It relates to educational orientation in the whole school because it can serve as the setting for good religious education, followed by its specific orientation.

The collection of focal points leads to some preliminary perspectives in section 3.

1. Dutch educational system and open Protestant-Christian schools

We have to go back to the nineteenth and early twentieth centuries for the genesis of the present Dutch educational system. For many years Orthodox, Protestants and Catholics lobbied for freedom of education. This was achieved in 1920, when a dual educational system was enshrined in Dutch law. In this dual system, education provided by the state and education organised by parents, were given equal status before the law. Until the latter part of the last century, children from Orthodox Protestant and Catholic families attended schools of their own denomination. Children of parents not belonging to either of these two religious groups sent their children to state-run primary schools with a more neutral ideology.

The current situation is quite different. The Christian population of today is very secularised. With the influx of people from many different cultures Dutch society has become pluralistic, like that in other West-European countries. The character of state-run schools in the Netherlands has also changed over the years. These schools no longer seek to take a neutral stance, but are 'actively pluriform', promoting knowledge and fellowship in the field of ideology. Religious education based on a particular tradition can be offered in all primary schools as an optional subject. As a result, children in all schools can do religious education if their parents wish them to do so. Moreover, local churches and mosques are invited to provide religious education. This usually amounts to one lesson a week. There is a similar arrangement for humanism, which is also an optional subject. However, both disciplines continue to be vulnerable because of the lack of funding and proper staffing.

Although one would expect that the greatest proportion of pupils would go to actively multiform state-run schools, in view of the secularisation and ideological plurality in Dutch society, in fact there has been an equal spread of pupils among the different types of schools for many years, with the result that each type of school receives one-third of the Dutch primary-school population. Most of the schools – regardless of ideology –, are chosen by children with diverse ideological backgrounds, although this is particularly the case in urban areas. At the same time, most Protestant-Christian schools now have an open-door policy for admission, while expecting non-religious parents to respect the school's religious ideology. A recent study (Dijkstra & Miedema, 2003) shows that parents are positive about the religious dimension of Protestant-Christian education. For their part, schools pay particular attention to dialogue with other faiths, albeit in the context of their own Christian tradition. With their open-door admission policy and their espousal of interreligious perspectives, these schools are referred to as open Protestant-Christian schools.

Apart from the confessional religious dimension that causes parents to opt for a school in a particular tradition, all schools in the Netherlands are obliged to include education about religion in a broad and general sense. This is provided in a separate subject called 'religious and ideological movements' (geestelijke stromingen). In this subject children are taught about spiritual/religious phenomena such as rites, buildings and holy books. The legal requirement is based on the assumption that knowledge of different religious and ideological movements promotes understanding and fellowship among pupils from different backgrounds. Nevertheless this informative approach has not met the expectations of the legislature. Meanwhile, open Christian schools have been looking for ways to integrate other religions in their own educational concept (Westerman, 2001). As a result of the current debate on citizenship and the role of religion and religious education in the public domain, Siebren Miedema recently called for religious identity formation for all students in all schools (Miedema, 2005). This would entail the reframing of religious education in all schools.

Figure 1: The school system in the Netherlands

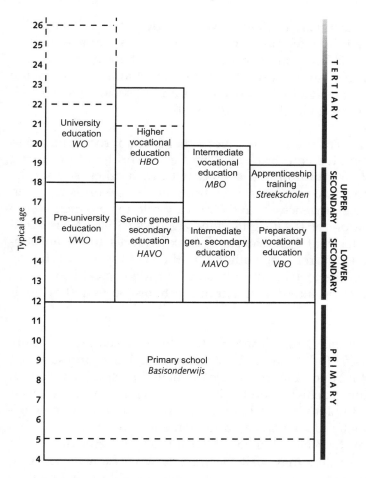

2. Methods and Examples of Good practice

Teaching Methods

This section contains a short description of three teaching methods widely used in religious education in the Netherlands. The methods are: *Kind op Maandag* (Child on Monday) and *Trefwoord* (Catchword). The third method *Hemel en Aarde* (Heaven and Earth) is new.

Kind op Maandag (Child on Monday)[1]: This method, which has been in use for thirty years, is published as periodical booklets and is regularly revised. The publication is aimed at teachers who wish to give meaning to the Protestant-Christian identity of the school. Teachers can use *Kind op Maandag* as well as their own individual background to develop their lessons. Each publication provides stories, visual material and teaching methods for all primary school classes.

Although the editorial team of *Kind op Maandag* does not give a specific statement of its objectives, reference is made to existing attainment targets for religious education in Protestant-Christian schools. The subject areas are: a) religious consciousness and knowledge of the Christian tradition; b) life questions and customs; c) ideological encounters and d) socio-ethical development. The method is used in about 1250 schools.

Trefwoord (Catchword)[2]: The method involves a thematic approach, linked to Bible stories. The objective is to bring the children's world and the world of the Jewish-Christian tradition into contact with each other, so that the children can learn from two perspectives by bringing these worlds together. First, the children use experiences from their own world to help them to understand the Bible. Secondly, the insights gained from the Bible help the children to discover the depth of their everyday life experiences. In this encounter, the children also learn from each other with the objective of developing an open view of life. The focus is on religious and ideological instruction in Protestant, Catholic and interdenominational schools. Some 1500 schools use this method.

Hemel en Aarde (Heaven and Earth)[3]: There are five theme-based projects, published in magazine form, for autumn, Christmas, winter, Easter and summer. The concrete subject matter includes the sea, money, time and Jerusalem. A deeper understanding is achieved on the basis of the children's experience. There is a subsequent link to the world of the Christian- and other ideological traditions. The material contains an arrangement of different texts that includes stories from the Bible. Users are referred to Children's Bibles. For further information, readers may visit the website www.hemelenaarde.nl. It contains supplementary information on the content and teaching method for specific lessons. Catholic schools are the main users of the *Hemel en Aarde* method. About 400 schools use the method.

---

1 Berger, U. & Nijenhuis, M. (Eds.) *Kind op Maandag [Child on Monday]*. Religious education method for primary schools (Amersfoort, NZV Uitgevers).
2 van 't Hof, L. (Ed.) *Trefwoord [Catchword]*. Teaching method for religious and world view education (Hoevelaken, SGO).
3 Deen, R. & Benjamins, R. (Eds.) *Hemel en Aarde [Heaven and Earth]*. Teaching method for religious and world view education in primary schools.

Reference framework 1: school-wide educational orientation

To assess the quality of the above methods, we have provided an outline of a dual reference framework,[4] of which the different aspects are listed under two headings: In this section we deal with school-wide educational orientation and in the next section with domain-specific orientation.

The first refers to the extended educational perspective. This perspective, which is less common in the Netherlands, allows religious education to become an integrated part of the regular educational curriculum. Though religious education may have a particular profile, the status of 'educational apartheid' within the school is not acceptable. It is a subject like any other and not a 'foreign matter' within the school.

Under the second heading, domain-specific orientations can contribute to the professional identification of 'good practice' in religious education.

Learning community: In using the term 'good practice' we think first about specific practice based on the personal qualities of individual teachers, rather than individual representations of good practice. We place the educational task of teachers in an extended rather than a restricted perspective. Responsibility for cohesive cognitive and socio-emotional learning processes should be based on a shared educational concept characterised by clear orientation towards development. This can contribute to continuous improvements in educational provision that includes religious education.

The principle of working from a shared concept presumes the existence of a 'community of learners'; that is a school where the focus is on pupils, teachers and parents who are brought together for the permanent enhancement of learning activity. Where this is the case, the school becomes a 'meeting place'. It is also an institute of knowledge as well as of social learning, a living community, where, at least in theory, pupils and teachers can fulfil their true potential. Such a community, where teachers and pupils gain useful knowledge by working together, is the first precondition for the achievement of 'good practices'. Furthermore, the idea of a 'community of learners' is also related to the professional development of teachers. The continuous challenge to improve the quality of education requires lifelong learning.

Emmaus model: The view of the school as an open meeting place highlights the importance of high-quality communication and educational processes. Within the Christian tradition The Walk to Emmaus (Lk 24:13), demonstrates the principle. The story describes the learning process of two pupils and their teacher. Insofar as this travel story is a metaphor for education, the learning process actually consists of four consecutive challenges:

---

4 This reference framework corresponds with recent didactical conceptions at the Primary Teacher Training Department of Windesheim University.

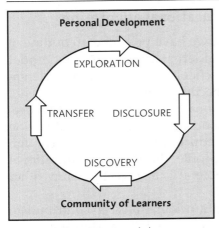

Figure 2: Emmaus model

- the exploration of authentic 'life questions';
- the disclosure of new ways of seeing based on reality;
- the discovery of new ways of acting;
- the transfer to new ways of being.

If learning in school is specifically focussed on these sequential challenges, the acquisition of theoretical knowledge can no longer be an end in itself. Only when knowledge is considered essential, elementary and relevant for pupils can it also be relevant and useful with a meaning for life. To quote Mahatma Gandhi: 'All our learning or recitation of the Vedas, correct knowledge of Sanskrit, Latin, Greek, and what not, will avail us nothing if they do not enable us to cultivate absolute purity of heart. The end of all knowledge must be building up of character.' (Gandhi, 1932)

Knowledge and Learning: The quotation from Mahatma Gandhi relates not only to the educational quality of knowledge, but also to the quality of the learning process necessary for personal meaning and interpretation. Both aspects are related and this is outlined briefly below.

Mahatma Gandhi's view and the promotion of identity development as the ultimate goal (the end) of knowledge acquisition, requires a critical examination of the quality of the school curriculum. An interesting benchmark is the criterion of inherent educational quality. We can refer to the argument of Kessels and Korthagen (1995) that education should not focus primarily on the reproduction of abstract, conceptual knowledge (epistèmè), but on the learner's perception of knowledge (phronèsis) which focuses on values, meaning and application (cf. Valstar, 1996). The actual integration of new knowledge depends on the learner's perception and interpretation. Meaning is not an objective characteristic of the subject matter. In theory, the learner attaches perception and meaning to the subject matter.

The educational quality of the learning process: The perception of the school as an open meeting place implies a specific approach to learning and instruction. The perception is illustrated in the Emmaus model. The four consecutive steps in the model are in line with current concepts of which the chief focus is on teaching pupils to learn (the learning-to-learn concept). Pupils and their learning needs are the subject of the individual learning process. An example of this approach is found in the entirety of current conceptions that tend

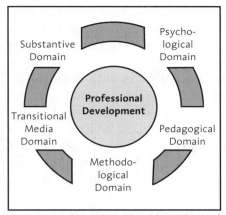

Figure 2: The educational quality of the learning process

to be termed social constructivism.[5] As a learning paradigm, the spectrum of social constructivism offers a challenging framework for educational innovation in general and developmental processes in particular. The paradigm is, at least in the Netherlands, an important inspirational source for innovation in teacher training study programmes and for educational publishers. In the development of school concepts and methods, people tend to fall back on elementary aspects of this paradigm. This is already happening in primary schools. It seems fair to assume that the paradigm of social constructivism will eventually become a reference point for the reform of concepts and school methods, including, of course, religious education.

In sum, we consider the perspective of the school as a learning community, the steps of the Emmaus model, pedagogical attention to the individual development of pupils and corresponding views on knowledge and learning, to be school-wide orientations in achieving better quality education. In anticipation of future developments, we will take account of social constructivism in our quest for 'good practice'.

Reference Framework 2: Domain-specific orientations

In following on from school-wide educational orientation, we will illustrate five mutually cohesive areas of a domain-specific nature for special attention. We also stress the necessity of supporting teachers in their professional development. In our view, the following points can serve as a second reference framework in the quest for 'good practice'.

1. The substantive domain: interpretation. In Protestant schools, the Christian tradition has essential meaning. This tradition is a guiding force in the development of educational perspectives. Religious traditions inspire and act as symbolic reference frameworks by which people give meaning to their lives in different ways (cf. Vergouwen 2001 and Kuindersma 1998). For us, this basic principle applies as much to the Christian tradition as to those of

---

5 Summarised: 1) Focus on the knowledge construction of the pupil as subject; 2) Attention for previous knowledge; 3) The use of multi-perspective views; 4) The inclusion of realistic and relevant contexts; 5) The positioning of knowledge in rich and complex learning environments; 6) The attention for self-responsibility and social interaction; 7) The development of self-awareness and reflection (cf Elizabeth Murphy, http://www.cdli. ca/~elmurphy/emurphy/cle.html).

other religions. What they have in common are multi-coloured patterns of life principles, experiences (of faith), ethical beliefs and moral practices, together with the sources of inspiration that underlie them. In this respect we have to deal with the particular issue of the correlation principle. The question is how the distinct and rich traditions and experiences of the past can be meaningfully linked to today's experiences.

In the Christian tradition, the Bible is regarded as a comprehensive source of reflection based on personal relationship with God. So biblical texts belong to the primary content in the educational process. The texts are not just material or assets for narratives, but also authentic literary documents that help pupils to discover meaning in life. A prerequisite is that pupils should be educated in how the world was then and that they should be guided as they discover the meaning of the religious language used in existential and critical situations at the time. Without that process it would be almost impossible to link biblical content to the world of pupils' current experience. Only when the correlation between traditions and actual reality is achieved, can the substantive process of interpretation be reached. A constructive learning process, as formulated by for example H.K. Berg[6], can then become an actual reality.

So the phenomenon of symbolic language is an illustration of a promising opportunity of opening up the Book of Books to pupils. Inspired by the dynamism of the symbolic-metaphoric layer of the Bible, many storytellers, poets, musicians, visual artists, theologians, philosophers and others have given form and content to what touched them in the tradition (history of reception). We also regard the totality of their personal inspiration, their creations and dilemmas and their moral view of the world and the way they lived their lives as essential material for the curriculum.

Finally, in considering the character of an open Christian school, it is obvious that interpretation and symbolic language are honoured in respect of other religious traditions.

2. The developmental-psychological domain: phases of development. By definition, the individual development of pupils is the focal point in their upbringing and education. The principle is pertinent to all subjects including religious education. In designing the learning process, it is essential for teachers to anticipate the various stages of development. Therefore, they must possess adequate pedagogical insight in general and knowledge of phases of (reli-

---

6 'In religious education the biblical content must be chosen and explained in such a way that young people recognize and learn the critical and liberating dynamics and unrelenting power of hope. Young people should be equipped to be able to critically analyse their own lives and the world around them, so that they can recognize and accept the liberating impulses of the biblical tradition as an opportunity to change.' ('Grundriß der Bibeldidaktik Konzepte – Modelle – Methoden', H. K. Berg, 1993. Also by the same author: Ein Wort wie Feuer. Wege lebendiger Bibelauslegung, 1995.)

gious) development in particular. In the first instance, this is required if they are to recognise the point at which pupils start to ask critical questions. Even though the symbolic-metaphoric language of religious traditions is conducive to this, children do not experience faith exclusively based on experiences and images. Sooner or later they approach religious education from a rational point of view. So their critical questions on matters such as meaning, truth and validity should be adequately discussed. Questions may be based on misconceptions and misunderstandings related to a specific phase of development. Then, knowledge is required of the stages of development important in selecting subject matter such as stories, texts, images and songs, while specific media may help children to cross thresholds or enable their further development. Finally, knowledge of concepts in stages of development enables teachers to gain insight into pupils' moral development, it also helps them in their own understanding of symbols. This insight may help them as they guide children in their transition from a literal to a more symbolic language of faith.

3. *The pedagogical domain: development of personal identity.* For a very long time, a dominant approach has been the transfer of religious stories and articles of faith in Protestant-Christian schools. The socialisation of children in the religious convictions of their parents and religious community was more or less automatic. Today, however, a religious upbringing and a supporting environment no longer exist. Children live in an ideological multiform and pluralistic environment, where they have to learn to understand themselves in the socio-emotional sense and where they have to find their own place. So, the basis of upbringing has changed. The emphasis no longer lies primarily in the transfer, but in the need for meaning and the development of personal identity[7]. With identity development in the educational sense we mean becoming a subject that is to reach personal stability and continuity as a person, together with appreciation of the importance of reflective insight into one's own place in society, history and culture.

The implication is that teachers must realise the pedagogical dimension of their task by helping pupils dialogically to integrate experience and new insight and to make personal choices (cf. Leeman & Wardekker 2004). In the general framework of socio-emotional development, this involves a range of composite skills. They include self-awareness, social awareness, self-management, responsible decision making and skills of relationship (CASEL, 2004). A specific focus on the development of the spiritual-human domain of identity is an essential characteristic for religious education. It is related to the development of a response to the spiritual dimension of existence – the focus on the relationship with God and humankind and the fundamental

---

7 Cf. Leeman, Y. & Wardekker, W. (2004) *Onderwijs met pedagogische kwaliteit* (Windesheim University).

experience of compassion. Within this framework it is essential to pay attention to self-image and self-esteem.

4. The methodological domain: active learning. An educational method is not an objective in itself, but a means of achieving objectives. In our view, the learning steps of the Emmaus model (exploration, disclosure, discovery and transfer) could act as a general framework to developing useful processes of active and involved learning. As indicated earlier, we see the school as a dynamic learning and living community. It is, therefore, important to transform teaching methods that force children to sit quietly, to listen and to imitate, so as to initiate new forms of authentic and social learning. This could be achieved through, for example, the ideas of social constructivism (see note 5). If mutual encounter takes centre stage, both pupils and teachers can actively play their own roles. Teachers bear personal responsibility for their educational task, including that of religious education. They should therefore implement a varied approach that allows for active participation and reflection. Examples of teaching methods are aspects of silence and action, narration and playing, text, images and music. Active involvement is a prerequisite to disclosing the reflective dimension of interpretation (cf. Kuindersma, 1998). In theory, we regard cohesive forms of participation and reflection, together with narration and ritualisation as the proprium and the methodological heart of religious education in the 21st century.

5. The transitional media domain: various mediators. The Christian tradition is primarily about the experience of faith that is about how people experience their relationship with God. Learning arrangements with a special focus on disclosure and discovery are required so as to involve children in these experiences. The effect of these kinds of learning arrangements depends strongly on the dynamic qualities of the media. The Dutch theologian Dingemans calls these particular media 'mediators' (Dingemans, 2000). They mediate between humankind, religion and God. Mediators can have the character of transitional objects, i.e. media that bring closer the mystery of transcendence. According to Dingemans, mediators can take various forms such as persons, stories, songs, music, images, symbols, prayers, silence, play and musicals. These mediators increasingly relate to symbolic language and symbolic acts that create space for human imagination and for experiencing the mystery of God. There are also aspects related to hermeneutics, for example media or incentives that will help children and youth to understand the world of religion and faith. Examples of these instruments are (for instance) a relevant case study, informative reference books and videos, that is everything that interests pupils and effectively contributes to the exploration and disclosure of new ways of seeing and ways of being. Perhaps the most important function of the methods of religious education lies in providing mediators.

Didactically, the presentation of the mediators should, in principle, relate to all the phases of educational provision. From the pedagogical perspective, mediators should fascinate and motivate pupils, in whatever way, to think about the world in the way it presents diverse forms of existence to them. When the mediators contain (multi-perspective) incentives, these can challenge the pupils to think critically about their own views and actions.

In this respect there is a current issue. Visual media are at least as important in the youth culture of today as textual matter. It is also extremely important that pupils use the functionality of electronic learning environments in religious education (actively and jointly). This includes web-based learning. So we need a substantial, policy-based investment in the expertise and the facilities the new e-teaching. Education in the Netherlands is highly dependent on current methods. That is why educational publishers are faced with the unenviable task of developing a total package of a wide range of media that will facilitate new learning activities. Teachers have few possibilities of developing these new mediators themselves. With few exceptions, most teachers will stick to the regular media offered by their religious education teaching method. Even in this case though, it should be understood that adequate mediators must be available with a distinctive theological, literary and aesthetic quality.

6. Teacher mentoring: professional development. It is essential that teachers be supported in the development and implementation of optimum learning processes. Experience has shown that it is almost impossible for teachers to take responsibility for this aspect of professional development in the limited time available. Gaining theological background information, identifying the context of Bible stories, knowledge of religions, etc. requires subject-specific expertise and support. It is asking too much of individual teachers to develop a totally new pedagogical format for their lessons a number of times a week. Religious teaching methods now offer all sorts of materials, although design and implementation in the classroom require a continuous learning process. Indeed, to reach the required level of school-wide and domain-specific expertise (see above) adequate professional support in the form of customised training is essential. Today, Dutch schools are involved in official collaborative relationships. This provides opportunities to invest in cross-school 'learning communities' that can contribute to the joint development of inspirational professional competence. Educational publishers and teacher training institutes should be able to offer their knowledge and teaching expertise. This is only happening occasionally at present.

3. Perspectives

The collection of focal points above leads one to some preliminary questions. We suppose that actual practice in religious education – insofar as it is inspired by the three methods, will not automatically be linked to an explicit school-wide concept. At best, possibilities for such a link have rarely been identified. This is surprising in the light of the prominent position that Protestant-Christian education gives to the ideological identity, – including the related pedagogical and educational identity.

The low level of attention paid to school-wide orientation also raises the questions as to whether the designers of methods are aware of the publications of the endowed chair of Protestant Education.

Each of the three methods has its own strengths. Nevertheless, these strengths could become a snare because of their relatively one-sided character. Attention to what is traditional can result in undervaluing the educational value of the pupils' participation. Conversely, the contribution of the traditional could suffer because of the attention given to socio-emotional development. In the same vein, undervaluing the developmental stages of the pupil is both general and striking. This also applies to cultural heritage when traditional historical perceptions are not dealt with.

The place and function of the Bible raise questions in all three methods. In the case of explicit biblical teaching methods, and the practical use of texts, teachers are given minimum or even no support. On the other hand, there is a perception that in recent times more attention is being given to the quality of the material and the individual pupil's participation. This applies to the area of experience, such as imagination, fantasy and creativity as well as in respect of reflection. In other words, we have found promising signs of good practice in the three methods.

Finally we refer here to the perhaps most urgent matter that arises from our first analyses: the quality of the correlation.

The relationship and balance between the pupil's experiences and tradition deserves a new and deeper reflection and a valid pedagogical concept and justification.

References

Berger, U. & Nijenhuis, M. (Eds.) (1982-1992) *Kind op Maandag [Child on Monday]*. Method for religious education in primary schools (Amersfoort, NZV).

Berg, H. K. (1993) *Grundriß der Bibeldidaktik Konzepte – Modelle – Methoden [Compendium of Bible Didactics. Concepts – Models – Methods]* (München/Stuttgart).

Berg, H. K. (1995) *Ein Wort wie Feuer. Wege lebendiger Bibelauslegung [A word like fire. Methods of creative Bible interpretation]* (München/Stuttgart).

Berg, S. (1995) *Kreative Bibelarbeit in Gruppen. 16 Vorschläge [Creative Bible work in Groups. 16 Proposals]* (München/Stuttgart).

Bucher, A. A., Büttner, G., Freudenberger-Lötz, P. & Schreiner, M. (Eds.) (2002) *Mittendrin ist Gott. Kinder denken nach über Gott, Leben und Tod [God is in the Centre. Children reflect about God, Life and Death]* Jahrbuch für Kindertheologie 1 (Stuttgart, Calwer).

Bucher, A. A., Büttner, G., Freudenberger-Lötz, P. & Schreiner, M. (Eds.) (2003) *Im Himmelreich ist keiner sauer. Kinder als Exegeten [In Heaven nobody is sulky. Children as exegetes]* Jahrbuch für Kindertheologie 2 (Stuttgart, Calwer).

CASEL, *Collaborative for Academic, Social, and Emotional Learning*, UIC Chicago, www.casel. org.

Dijkstra, A. B. & Miedema, S.,(2003) *Bijzonder gemotiveerd*. Een onderzoek naar de ideale school volgens dragers en vragers van confessioneel basisonderwijs (Assen).

Dingemans, G. D. J. (2000) *De stem van de roepende* (Kampen).

Liesbeth van 't Hof (Ed.) *Trefwoord [Catchword]*. Method for religious education and world view education (Hoevelaken, SGO).

Westerman, W. (2001) *Ongewenste objectiviteit*. Onderwijs in geestelijke stromingen in historisch en vergelijkend perspectief (Kampen).

Deen, R. & Benjamins, R. (Eds.) *Hemel en Aarde [Heaven and Earth]*. Method for religious education and world view education in primary schools (Amersfoort, Kwintessens).

Gandhi, M. (1932) *Weekly Journal Young India*, February 1932.

Kessels, J. P. A. M. & Korthagen, F. A.J. (1995) *The relationship between theory and practice*. Paper Annual Meeting ATEE Oslo.

Kuindersma, H. (1998) *Godsdienstige communicatie met kinderen door symbooltaal* (Kampen).

Leeman, Y. A. M. & Wardekker, W. L. (2004) *Onderwijs met pedagogische kwaliteit* (Zwolle, Windesheim University).

Miedema, S. (2005) *Religious identity formation for all students & in all schools*. Paper Annual Meeting EAWRE Amsterdam.

Valstar, J. G. (1996) Het perspectief en de ontwikkeling van waarden, in: D. van Veen & W. Veugelers (Eds.) *Vernieuwing van leraarschap en lerarenopleiding* (Leuven/Apeldoorn), 113-122.

Valstar, J. G. (2004) Naar een integrale benadering van de Pedagogische Opdracht, in: G. ten Dam, W. Vleugelers, W. Wardekker & S. Miedema (Eds.) *Pedagogisch opleiden/De pedagogische taak van de lerarenopleidingen* (Amsterdam), 103-120.

Vergouwen, C. G. (2001) *Een hemelsbrede gelijkenis. Geloofsopvoeding in godsdienstpsychologisch perspectief* (Kampen).

Winnips, J. C. (1998) *Scaffolding the development of skills in the design process for educational media through hyperlinked units of learning material*. (Internal report) (Enschede, University of Twente, The Netherlands).

'Enriched Religious Education' in Primary Schools in Northern Ireland

James Nelson

Introduction

In recent years teaching and learning in Primary schools in Northern Ireland has been reinvigorated through a thorough review of the whole Primary school curriculum. An effort has been made to empower pupils and teachers in the learning and teaching process by allowing greater independence, creativity and flexibility. Learning is being made more enjoyable and meaningful through a curriculum which is coherent and based on broad themes and transferable skills rather than individual subject disciplines. And schooling for young children in particular is being released from a constraining formalism to allow structured play to become the core learning methodology. This chapter provides an example of how religious education is being taught successfully and innovatively in such a learning context for four to six year olds; the example is *Enriched Religious Education (RE)*. But, to begin with, it is important to place the example in its context and provide an overview of religious education in Primary schools in Northern Ireland.

1. The Education System, Primary Schools and Religious Education

The teaching of religious education in Primary Schools in Northern Ireland has emerged from a contentious and fractious history that is closely bound up with religious exclusivism, sectarian politics and social conflict. At the formation of Northern Ireland's educational structures in the 1920's there was an attempt to establish common schools, open to all children, through a strict separation of religious education from secular instruction (The Londonderry Education Act 1923). All children were to receive common secular education while religious education would take place outside formal school hours, however, political opposition and social forces (including the vociferous protests of all the main Christian denominations) were such that in a short space of time the system fragmented along religious lines: Catholic schools for Catholic children and state Controlled schools for all others - a predominantly Protestant population who insisted on Protestant clerical representation on the management boards of these fully funded state schools.

Broadly speaking, today there are schools of three different management types in Northern Ireland: Controlled, Maintained and Integrated (McGlynn, 2004; Smith, 2001). All could be called state schools in the sense that they are funded, almost entirely, by the state but they each have a separate identity. Maintained schools are Catholic schools; Controlled schools are 'non-denominational' in ethos and cater for a largely Protestant population; and Integrated schools aim to bring together 'pupils, staff and governors, in roughly equal numbers, from Protestant, Catholic, other faiths and none,' within a Christian ethos (www.nicie.org).

Compulsory schooling in Northern Ireland begins when children are 4-5 years old, although over ninety percent of children now experience some form of pre-school education (DENI, 2005). This high participation in pre-school education has allowed curriculum planners to begin the first stage of the curriculum, the Foundation Stage, in pre-school settings (illustrated below). The Foundation Stage continues on into the Primary School in Years 1 and 2. (In this context it is important to note that pre-school settings are exempt from teaching religious education; Foundation Stage religious education does not begin until Year 1). After the Foundation Stage pupils progress through Key Stages 1 and 2 until, at age 11-12, they transfer to a Post-Primary school. Currently an academic selection system is in place which rewards those who pass a test called 'The Eleven Plus' with a place in a Grammar school, although this test is to be abolished from 2008. Pupils continue through Key Stages 3 and 4 at their Post-Primary school until the end of compulsory schooling in Year 12.

Figure 1: The school system in Northern Ireland

Age	Key Stage	Year	School
15-16	Key Stage 4	Year 12	Post-Primary Schools
14-15		Year 11	
13-14	Key Stage 3	Year 10	
12-13		Year 9	
11-12		Year 8	
10-11	Key Stage 2	Year 7	Primary Schools
9-10		Year 6	
8-9		Year 5	
7-8	Key Stage 1	Year 4	
6-7		Year 3	
5-6	Foundation Stage	Year 2	
4-5		Year 1	
3-4			Pre-school settings (Nursery schools, reception classes in Primary Schools, Playgroups etc.)

Religious Education in Primary Schools

Despite their differences, all three school sectors (Controlled, Maintained and Integrated) in Northern Ireland teach a compulsory common syllabus of religious education (DENI, 1993) – although it is fair to say that the actual implementation of the syllabus varies greatly in relation to content, resources and teaching methodologies from sector to sector. *The Northern Ireland Core Syllabus for Religious Education* (DENI, 1993) was designed by the four largest Christian denominations in Ireland (Roman Catholic, Church of Ireland, Presbyterian and Methodist) and involves a study of Christianity under three Attainment Targets: The Revelation of God, The Challenge of Jesus and The Christian Church. The syllabus is underpinned by Christian values and the assumption that it is designed to encourage Christian spirituality in children (Nelson, 2004).

In *Controlled Primary Schools* most teachers teach religious education as part of the statutory curriculum. Legislation asserts that religious education in grant-aided (Controlled) schools 'shall be undenominational religious education, that is to say, education based upon the Holy Scriptures according to some authoritative version or versions thereof...' (HMSO, 1986:article 21.2). There is also a conscience clause in the legislation relating to the teaching of religious education which allows a teacher to request exemption, although only a small minority exercise this right. Up-to-date statistical information on the frequency of religious education lessons or the percentage of curriculum time given over to religious education is not available but it is fair to say that practice varies widely and also depends on what is understood as 'religious education'. Some schools might include Assembly (an act of collective worship) as part of the time allocated to religious education, while others regard religious education to be specific lessons dedicated to the delivery of the Core Syllabus. While Controlled schools have a mainly Protestant Christian heritage they lack an agreed set of explicit values and so vary greatly in the extent to which they possess a Christian, Protestant, religiously inclusive or secular ethos.

All Controlled Primary schools should have a teacher responsible for co-ordinating religious education which involves maintaining schemes of work across the primary school, coordinating the school's religious education resources, acquiring and disseminating new resources and keeping informed of new developments in the subject through attendance at in-service training. In some cases this teacher has received specialist training in religious education as part of his or her initial degree.

The religious education resources used by Primary School teachers in Controlled schools tend to be photocopiable worksheets on biblical stories provided by the five Education and Library Boards of Northern Ireland.

The majority of Controlled Primary Schools have long-established links with clergy of local Protestant churches. In some cases these clergy conduct occasional religious education lessons and they frequently participate in school assemblies. Clergy also have the right to inspect the teaching of religious education in Controlled schools and this role is exercised by a few; generally, churches prefer to see their task as building relationships with schools and offering support in the overall provision of religious education.

In *Catholic Maintained Primary Schools* religious education is regarded as an integral part of the whole curriculum; schooling is regarded as 'both, and simultaneously, a sacred and secular activity which requires synthesis of both elements for a genuine authentic philosophy of education.' (The Catholic Bishops of Northern Ireland 2001:4) While there is a sense in which everything that is taught in Catholic schools contributes to the religious education of the children there is also provision for specific religious education lessons. This generally follows the Diocesan catechetical programme *Alive-O* which consists of a series of pupil and teacher books as well as other support materials such as CD-ROMs and videos published by the Veritas publishing house in Dublin. The programme covers the majority of the content of the Core Syllabus as well as going beyond it to include material directly related to Catholic sacramental preparation. Undoubtedly, faith development is a foundational and explicit aim of religious education in Catholic schools.

The teaching of religious education in Maintained schools is coordinated by a teacher, some of whom studied religious education as a main component of their initial teacher education, but all of whom have received a Catholic Certificate in Religious Education as part of their initial degree. Catholic Clergy also play an important part in religious education through assisting in the preparation of children for receiving the Christian sacraments of Reconciliation, First Communion and Confirmation. The clergy also work closely with the principal and religious education coordinator to ensure appropriate standards in religious education are maintained.

Integrated schools are Christian in ethos, but due to the religiously mixed nature of their pupil population the teaching of religious education has always provided a challenge for parents, teachers and school management teams. It is a challenge that has demanded creative thinking and careful planning in order to address sensitive issues over providing catechetical teaching for children of some Christian denominations while teaching religious education to religiously mixed groups in accordance with the Integrated Education Movement's spirit of togetherness. Practical guidelines on religious education in Integrated schools have been produced by the Northern Ireland Council for Integrated Education (NICIE) but these are basic principles and are not prescriptive in relation to organisation or timetabling of the subject. For example, they state:

> The children shall learn together all that we can reasonably expect them to learn together.

And

> Where the school population includes significant numbers of children of a particular religious community, separate provision should be made to prepare such children for sacramental and liturgical participation in that specific religious community if their parents so wish… (NICIE 2001:24).

An internal report (NICIE RE Focus Group, 2002) based on responses to a questionnaire from teachers in 20 Integrated primary schools highlighted wide variations in the time allocated to religious education (from 30 mins to 2 hrs 30 mins per week), the resources used, the content of lessons and the arrangements for catechetical teaching. There is no doubt that the situation is still evolving with varied practice across the Integrated sector.

Examples of resources used include the Alive O series, mentioned above, (or material adapted from it) in religious education lessons with Catholic children and Delving Deeper (NICIE, 2005) in religious education lessons with Protestant children. A combination of materials from other sources is used for teaching other children or for times of shared religious education.

Similar to other sectors, each Integrated school has a religious education co-ordinator. Most members of staff will contribute to the teaching of religious education in some form by taking a time of shared religious education, Protestant religious education or Catholic religious education, depending on the teacher's own beliefs and what arrangements are in place in the school. In many cases Protestant clergy assist with the delivery of Protestant religious education although Catholic clergy rarely visit an Integrated school as they believe their duty is to the Maintained school sector. Catholic catechetical instruction is delivered by Catholic teachers who have completed a Catholic Certificate in Religious Education.

Recent Reforms

At the time of writing, a review of the Primary School Curriculum in Northern Ireland is ongoing (Northern Ireland Council for the Curriculum Examinations and Assessment (CCEA), 2002). This review is being managed by the Northern Ireland Council for Curriculum, Examinations and Assessment (CCEA) which has responsibility for the whole curriculum, except for religious education. The aim of the review is to improve the balance, coherence and flexibility of the Northern Ireland curriculum at each Key Stage recognising recent developments in technology, educational research and the changing nature of society. In particular, it is intended that subjects will be brought together into learning areas, there will be a greater emphasis on transferable skills, a new approach to early years' education will be developed and the personal development of pupils will become part of the formal curriculum.

As well as the CCEA review of the Primary School curriculum, a review of the Core Syllabus for Religious Education has also taken place and a revised Core Syllabus agreed (DENI, 2006). At Primary School level there is little that is different from the previous syllabus. The most significant change is the division of what was previously Key Stage 1 into two learning stages: The Foundation Stage and Key Stage 1. In effect, the basic content has remained unchanged.

2. Methods and Example of Good Practice

The example of good practice in religious education from Northern Ireland which I wish to present is *Enriched RE*. This is an approach which aims to develop in children creative, open and reflective responses to religious education. The context of the example is early years' education and the teaching of religious education using an Enriched Curriculum approach. I will begin with a brief description of the need for change and the catalyst for change before turning to consider *Enriched RE* in practice.

A movement to reform early years' education in the Primary School in Northern Ireland emerged around 1999. The motivation was to learn from the best experiences and research of early years' education from around the world and to implement a child-centred approach which moved the focus in teaching and learning from curriculum content to the child; from learning *about* to learning *through* (Crowe, 2004). The project took the name 'Enriched Curriculum' and has been piloted with significant success in 31 schools around Northern Ireland (CCEA, 2002).

Pedagogical principles and pedagogical strategies

To understand the nature of the Enriched Curriculum further it is useful to distinguish between *pedagogical principles* and *pedagogical strategies* (Grimmitt, 2000). One of the features of the pilot study is the strong emphasis on its underlying principles; teachers who speak about the Enriched Curriculum often prefer to describe it as an *ethos* or *approach* and see it as a *process* rather than the implementation of a static curriculum (BELB, 2002). The pedagogical principles central to the Enriched Curriculum were distilled into four underlying principles by teachers working on the project. These could be summarised as: (1) providing a safe, secure and inviting learning environment where children feel valued; (2) utilising every opportunity to promote children's self-esteem, confidence, independence, imagination and general well-being; (3) allowing children's individual learning preferences to inform teacher planning and so increase the amount of significant learning taking place; (4) empowering teachers to use their own professional judgement in designing appropriate learning opportunities (BELB, 2002).

These pedagogical principles have taken form in a range of pedagogical strategies such as structured play, circle time[1], games, story-telling and literacy activities, practical numeracy activities and creative and expressive activities through art and music, which are employed as the teacher sees fit:

> In general teachers begin the day with a period of play for 1-1½ hours followed by snack and story time. The rest of the day is spent on practical maths activities, reading and writing opportunities, outdoor play, circle time, PE, music and drama. It is important to stress that the timetable varies from school to school. (BELB 2002:18)

The school environment has also had to change to adapt to these new learning styles. Where previously many Year 1 and 2 pupils spent a large part of their day behind desks they now have specific areas for play, a story corner and a writing area. Corridors and spare classrooms have been adapted to allow for greater movement and pupils are encouraged to be independent and, as far as possible, to make their own choices.

The results of the Enriched Curriculum seem to be very positive for both teachers and pupils with increased flexibility, creativity and enjoyment in the classroom. Teachers believe that the programme can help children develop greater concentration, better communication skills, increased confidence, improved leadership qualities and a greater sense of independence, self-esteem and responsibility (BELB, 2002).

Enriched RE in practice

On a simple level *Enriched RE* is the teaching of religious education using the Enriched Curriculum approach outlined above, but it is fair to ask what this means in practice. One teacher, Catherine Morrison, a Primary 1 teacher in Ballysillan Primary School, Belfast has been among a number of teachers who have been pioneering the teaching of religious education using an Enriched Curriculum approach. Ballysillan is a Controlled Primary School in the north of the city which has been involved in the Enriched Curriculum project since 2000. During the academic years 2002-03 and 2003-04, Catherine put specific effort into developing her teaching of religious education through the Enriched Curriculum approach. She believes it transformed her teaching:

> I feel the way we were teaching religious education was just telling a story, giving a worksheet and telling the children exactly what to do. We would say 'make sure you know that, then colour in the picture' and that was it. Now I want them to explore the material for themselves, I take my lead from them.

---

1   Circle time is a teaching method designed to enhance pupils' communication skills and personal development. See, for example, Mosle & Sonnet, 2001.

In practical terms *Enriched RE* has encouraged Catherine to introduce new methods and teaching strategies:

> My religious education is now very open-ended. I have an outcome which I want, for example for the children to explore a bible story and think about why the event happened, how it relates to them and the outside world, but I don't have only one task in mind. I wait to see where they take me with it – sometimes it involves discussion or structured play around the story or sometimes a role-play which can include making props and costumes or finger puppets. It is a better learning experience for the children and they enjoy it. The children also bounce ideas off each other. If one pupil says something another may say 'but...' and is prepared to challenge it. There is certainly more pupil interaction.

While the content of the syllabus has not been changed, the approach to teaching it is fundamentally different. Whereas before, a story/worksheet formula was standard, now learning objectives are set to emphasise skills and processes and these are facilitated through imaginative opportunities for playing, making, creating, interacting and responding. This change could be characterised as a move from a model of transmission to a model of trans-formation (Wardekker & Miedema, 2001). Rather than knowledge, skills and values being transmitted to children by their teacher the transformative view of education sees learning as fundamentally about participation:

> In such a transformation conception of education, learning is defined as the growing capacity or the growing competency of pupils to par-ticipate in culturally structured practices... In other words, being able to show that you 'know' the subject-matter is not the main criterion for a successful learning process; it is only the starting point for 'real' learning processes in which both the subject-matter and the learner are transformed. (Wardekker & Miedema 2001:80)

In practice, then, *Enriched RE* is about providing opportunities for children to encounter stories, people, places and events associated with religions in a way which encourages them to interact and respond through playing, mak-ing, creating, talking and thinking. This in turn allows religious education to move from a pedagogical model based on transmission to a model based on transformation; from a learning environment where meaning is given to one in which the learner participates and interacts with material in order to construct meaning (Grimmitt, 2000:chapter 11).

Working collaboratively the teacher above and author developed a plan-ning template (below) to assist other teachers interested in planning for *Enriched RE*. The examples given in the left hand column of the template are taken from the Northern Ireland curriculum and serve to illustrate possible learning outcomes in that context but the template could be easily adapted for use in other circumstances. The key elements of the template are content, learning objectives, activities and strategies, pupil initiated learning and reflection and evaluation. A brief discussion of each of these may help to further clarify the planning and implementation of *Enriched RE*.

Lesson	Intended Learning Outcome
Link to Core Syllabus – The Revelation of God – The Christian Church – Christian Morality OR **Link to learning beyond the Core Syllabus** – Sources of faith – People, places and practices – Issues of faith	**Pupils should learn about**
Link to Foundation Stage Skills Learning Skills – asking questions – observing using all senses – using imagination – investigating ideas – solving problems – making decisions – talking about their work/play – performing – developing visual and aural memory Social Skills – listening – working co-operatively – developing relationships – managing emotions and behaviour	**Pupils should learn how to**
Link to Foundation Stage Objectives (Awareness of Themselves, Others and the Environment): – confidence and self-esteem – awareness of emotions – awareness of personal safety – awareness of right and wrong – a sense of fairness and respect for others – a sense of wonder – mutual understanding of the feelings, emotions and lifestyles of others – care for classroom resources and respect for the environment	**Pupils should learn from this**

Activities/Strategies Role of Facilitators	Pupil-Initiated Learning	Resources
Reflection/Evaluation/Observation		

The statutory Core Syllabus for Northern Ireland (DENI, 1993) is the start-ing point for teachers when choosing the *content* of religious education les-sons. However, Catherine quickly realised that when using the Enriched Curriculum approach children did not confine their questions or ideas to a prescribed syllabus and there were themes and topics raised by the children which she wanted to pursue in future lessons. The need to go beyond the Core Syllabus in religious education in Northern Ireland has, in the past, been encouraged by the Inspectorate (ETI, 2000) and, helpfully, a model for how to do so has been developed by Richardson (2001). It was felt it would be helpful, therefore, to encourage teachers to allow themselves to go be-yond the core in their planning by including reference to Richardson's clas-sifications (Sources of faith; People, places and practices; Issues of faith) in the template.

In relation to *learning objectives* Grimmitt (1987; 2000) has provided a clas-sic, and now well known, breakdown of interactions in teaching religious education under the titles *learning about* religion and *learning from* religion. In an analysis of her teaching, Catherine felt that she had clearly moved from providing *learning about* interactions to including *learning from* interactions, but after some reflection she thought that the single heading *learning from* did not sufficiently do justice to the two distinct outcomes of skills and values held so centrally in the Enriched Curriculum approach and expressed in the Foundation Stage Proposals (CCEA, 2002). It was felt, therefore, that in the planning template it would be useful to set learning outcomes in skills-based learning, expressed as *learning how to,* as distinct from affective, values-based learning, expressed as *learning from.* An illustration of these learning objec-tives is given below.

Planning for Enriched RE

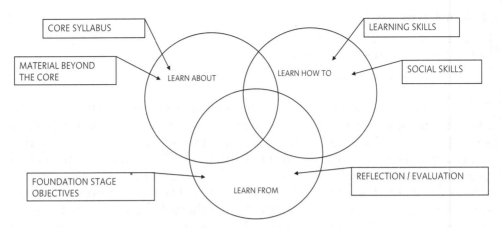

Key Principles

Teachers should:

1. provide a safe, secure and inviting learning environment where children feel valued
2. utilise every opportunity to promote children's self-esteem, confidence, independence, imagination and general well-being
3. allow children's individual learning preferences to inform teacher planning and so increase the amount of significant learning taking place
4. be empowered to use their own professional judgement in designing appropriate learning opportunities.

(Key Principles adapted from *The Enriched Curriculum BELB (2002)*)

When planning *activities and strategies* using an *Enriched RE* approach there will always be a degree of provisionality as it is accepted that while lessons are planned and led by teachers and classroom assistants the children are free to make choices and decisions about the activities they choose as the lesson progresses, so not everything is known in advance. However, all activities and strategies offered should be child-centred and based on encouraging play, talking and listening skills, creativity, problem solving and decision-making.

Teachers and classroom assistants do not lead and command but facilitate and guide children as they engage in the activities. Again, this is reflected in the planning template which provides a space to highlight the *role of the facilitators*. This could include particular prompts used to initiate the learning process or the practical assistance on offer for a particular activity within the room or a specific supervision requirement.

An example of a structured activity organised by the class teacher was a Christian wedding. All pupils had a role – from bride and groom to wedding guests; costumes were hired and the classroom arranged to host a wedding reception. While this activity required a significant amount of organisation the *Enriched RE* approach was still central. As a result of the lesson it was intended pupils would learn about Christian weddings and what is involved in a marriage ceremony and wedding reception; learn how to use their imagination, perform, develop relationships with others, match their behaviour to the social setting, ask questions; learn from the experience confidence and self-esteem, awareness of others, awareness of the joy associated with marriage, reasons why marriage is important to Christians, some of their own views on marriage.

Pupils were involved right from the planning process and were encouraged to share any experiences of attending weddings and to talk about the idea of marriage. On the day of the event they participated in a simple ceremony and were free to play in their roles. Instead of just being told what Christian weddings involve the children were engaged in a kinaesthetic learning process in which they came to an understanding of the significance of a Christian wedding for themselves through participating in a re-enactment of the social and cultural practice.

It can be the case that lesson planning is regarded as an activity which begins and ends before the lesson, but the Enriched Curriculum encourages teachers to move away from thinking about planning, teaching and reflection as three distinct phases of teaching. Rather, they are three elements which continually occur as part of a single continuous process and which are constantly being reshaped and modified by the teacher through her interaction with planning materials, resources, dialogue with other colleagues and, most importantly, in interaction with the children. It would be impossible, and of dubious value, for a teacher to fully document this whole complex process but in devising the planning template it was felt that it should in some way reflect the fact that the *Enriched RE* approach is process based and that each lesson evolves as it is being delivered. As a result, a place is provided where the teacher can note aspects of pupil initiated learning which occur during the lesson. This can also be used to help inform assessment as well as future planning.

An important element of the Enriched Curriculum approach is that it encourages pupils to reflect and evaluate on their learning experience and, in a manner suitable to their age and ability level, acknowledge what they have learned and the extent to which they have enjoyed the process. This self-evaluation also provides the teacher with a vital opportunity to observe the progress of a child or group of children and help with the assessment of their needs. The relevant section of the planning template may be used, therefore, to plan opportunities for reflection and evaluation as well as to report on particular observations made during a lesson.

3. Perspectives

There is no doubt that the fine work being carried out by Catherine Morrison at Ballysillan Primary School is an example of good practice in religious education, but during the period of implementing the *Enriched RE* approach Catherine also became aware of some difficulties. Three areas of concern in particular were the recording of progress, resources and the lack of diversity in the content material.

The issue of recording pupils' progress raised fundamental issues about what observations should be recorded and how they were to be assessed. Catherine feels the development of the lesson planning template has gone some way to solving this problem although questions still remain over how to classify progress, particularly in relation to the development of moral character and spiritual awareness (two objectives mentioned in the Foundation Stage Proposals (CCEA, 2002)). This is clearly an area where further work and research would be helpful.

As with implementing any new teaching programme for the first time it was essential to develop new resources. This was a recurring difficulty for Catherine but one which she responded to with creativity and imagination. However, she felt resource related problems might be reduced through teachers working together collectively to share ideas and resources from an *Enriched RE* approach. An alternative solution is adapting material from other projects which share a similar learning style and Catherine is currently exploring how she might adapt resources from the 'Godly Play' approach (Berryman, 1991) with her children.

Catherine found that by basing her lessons on the Northern Ireland Core Syllabus (DENI, 1993) the content was always within the Christian tradition. This placed limitations on the exploration of diverse religious traditions and cultures in her use of *Enriched RE*. The inadequacy of this was further highlighted when a Muslim child joined the class. Catherine has since taken it upon herself to explore material beyond the Core Syllabus in her religious education. However, it is disappointing that in the revised Core Syllabus for religious education in Northern Ireland (DENI, 2006) the content of Primary School religious education remains narrowly Christian.

Despite these difficulties it is hoped that the excellent *Enriched RE* developing in Ballysillan Primary School and other Primary Schools can influence practice across the region and generate an approach to the teaching of religious education that is open, investigative and relevant and takes account of the need for the development of knowledge, skills and values.

References

Belfast Education and Library Board (BELB) (2002) *Enriched Curriculum: the beginning* (Belfast, Belfast Education and Library Board).

Berryman, J. (1991) *Godly Play* (Minneapolis, Augsburg).

Crowe, L. (2004) *Enriching the Curriculum* (http://www.belb.org.uk/teachers/earlyCurriculumProgramme.asp?ddid=172#2 [accessed 18 June, 2004]).

Department of Education Northern Ireland (DENI) (1993) *Core Syllabus for Religious Education* (Bangor, DENI).

Department of Education Northern Ireland (DENI) (2005) *Children in Pre-School Places* (http://www.deni.gov.uk/facts_figures/elb_04_05/board_funded_pre_school_places.pdf [accessed 18 May, 2005]).

Department of Education Northern Ireland (DENI) (2006) *Proposals for a Revised Core Syllabus for Religious Education in Grant-Aided Schools in Northern Ireland* (Bangor, DENI).

Education and Training Inspectorate (ETI) (2000) *Evaluating Religious Education* (http://www.deni.gov.uk/inspection_services/inspection_related_publications/RE2000.pdf [accessed 2 April, 2004]).

Grimmitt, M. (1987) *Religious Education and Human Development* (Great Wakering, Essex, McCrimmon Publishing).

Grimmitt, M. (2000) *Pedagogies of Religious Education* (Great Wakering, Essex, McCrimmon Publishing).

HMSO (1986) *The Education and Libraries* (Northern Ireland) Order 1986 (Belfast, HMSO).

McGlynn, C. (2004) *Diversity of School Provision in Northern Ireland – Co-existence or Integration?* (Paper presented at Annual Conference of the Educational Studies Association of Ireland, Maynooth).

Mosley, J. & Sonnet, H. (2001) *Here We Go Round: Quality Circle Time For 3-5 Year Olds* (Trowbridge, Positive Press).

Nelson, J. (2004) Uniformity and Diversity in Religious Education in Northern Ireland, *British Journal of Religious Education*, 26 (3), 249-258.

Northern Ireland Council for Integrated Education (NICIE) (2001) *What's What in Integrated Education... A Guide for Teachers* (Belfast, NICIE publications).

NICIE RE Focus Group (2002) *Primary School Questionnaire: a summary of findings* (Belfast, Northern Ireland Council for Integrated Education (NICIE)).

Northern Ireland Council for Integrated Education (NICIE) (2005) *Delving Deeper* (Belfast, NICIE).

Northern Ireland Council for the Curriculum Examinations and Assessment (CCEA) (2002) *Detailed Proposals for the Revised Primary Curriculum and its Assessment Arrangements* (Belfast: Northern Ireland Council for the Curriculum, Examinations and Assessment (CCEA)).

Richardson, N. (2001) *Teaching Religion in a Conflictual Society* (Paper presented at European Network for Conflict Resolution in Education (ENCORE), Bosnia).

Smith, A. (2001) Religious Segregation and the Emergence of Integrated Schools in Northern Ireland, *Oxford Review of Education*, 27 (4), 559-575.

The Catholic Bishops of Northern Ireland (2001) *Proclaiming the Mission* (Armagh, The Catholic Bishops of Northern Ireland).

Wardekker, W. & Miedema, S. (2001) Identity, Cultural Change and Religious Education, *British Journal of Religious Education*, 23 (2), 76-87.

Differences in the Classroom – How to organise Religious Education in Norway?

Elisabeth K. Haanes and Heid Leganger-Krogstad[1]

Introduction: A Classroom Story

Mustafa was in the fifth grade (age 10) when I became his new teacher.[2] Mustafa often fought in the school yard, and it was easy to provoke him. Mustafa belongs to a refugee family that immigrated to the Oslo area from Iraq some years ago. He was the only Muslim student in his class in a school with only a few other Muslim. I decided to address Islam early this term as part of religious education. Mustafa who had been uninterested during lessons, woke up when I displayed objects and pictures as examples of Islamic calligraphy and ornamentation, he woke up. Under a cloth a prayer rug, a ceramic dish and a lamp were hidden and I unveiled them one by one. I demonstrated the endless multiplication of geometric and other patterns and showed them how they are permuted. I explained that this is done to give humans a feeling of continuous space and to remind us that Allah is eternal and raised above time. When they could study the objects more closely, they could discover themselves and discuss how the artisans had tried to depict the divine by weaving beautiful, repetitive patterns. At the beginning, Mustafa held back. But after a while, he took hold of the lamp and – in a voice that hardly could be heard he told the class that it was very much like one they had at home. One of the girls then burst out: 'Oh, it's so beautiful! Does your family have such a lamp?' Mustafa became enthusiastic. He touched the prayer rug and explained that his family had a similar rug. The reluctant and grudging boy was transformed into an enthusiastic member of the fellowship. He found out that the others were gathered around him commenting with wonder and admiration on all the items belonging to his tradition.

The story tells us about the effect of relating consciously to Mustafa's experience and background in a whole class setting as part of the lesson. When an item or subject is brought forward as part of the lesson for everyone to deal with, that functions as an important confirmation of its value. In Mustafa's case this could have been done in many other school subjects through use of his background in geography lessons, by making use of Iraqi stories, news, clothes, music or food and it could have had some of the same effect on him and his classmates. In religious education, however, this does not happen

---

1   Elisabeth K. Haanes, teacher in primary education, contributes with the stories from the classroom setting and reflections on planning, goals, motifs and experiences in this article (Birkedal & Haanes, 2003; E. Haanes, 2001; E. K. Haanes, 2003). Heid Leganger-Krogstad, teacher educator and researcher in philosophy of religious education, gives more of the background information (Afdal, Haakedal & Leganger-Krogstad, 2006 (1997); Leganger-Krogstad, 1997, 2000, 2001, 2003).

2   'I' in this text refers to Elisabeth K. Haanes.

occasionally only, but is systematically included in the multireligious subject matter introduced in 1997 in Norwegian schools.

1. School System, Primary School and Religious Education

Context

Up to 1975, when the current immigration began, Norway was a relatively homogenous society from a religious point of view. *Knowledge of Christianity* in school was catechetic education on behalf of the Church of Norway up to 1969. It was offered as an optional confessional subject according to the tenets of the Lutheran denomination, with a certain emphasis on common and ecumenical features in dividing issues. The Church of Norway is organised as a state church to which 86% of the population belong today. The total number of inhabitants is 4.6 million, Students outside this major church had the option of full exemption, and they were offered *Knowledge of World Views* as an alternative subject from 1974 on. Twenty years later 4% of the pupils made use of this alternative, and another 1% opted out without having any RE in schools. When 95% of the pupils took part in *Knowledge of Christianity*, it included pupils belonging to the Free Churches (2.4%), members of the major world religions, and pupils without religious affiliation. The alternative subject was secular-based and as such no good alternative for the Muslim community. An increasing number of Muslim pupils did not attend any religious education in schools. The school authorities realised the need for a change in the organisation of RE. Future models for RE had to meet the challenges of an increasingly multireligious globalised world. The crucial question for the authorities was: Is it possible to make RE a general and compulsory subject in a state school system like the Norwegian?

The public school system has a 'national function' in keeping together a young nation with a small and extremely scattered population (Skeie, 2006). The vast majority of children attend the public state school, which then is a neighbourhood school. Only 2.1% of all primary and lower secondary pupils attend non-state schools.[3] The state school is governed by egalitarian principles where permanent streaming of pupils according to ability or gender is not permitted by law. The education policy for schools follows an integrated approach, and special schools are kept to a minimum and most children attend their own home school. The pupils are kept together in classes through all stages with the aim to mirror the diversity in life outside school. In 1997 compulsory education in Norway was extended from nine to ten years, starting at the age of 6. Grade 1-7 is the primary stage and grade 8-10 the lower secondary stage of education. The class is regarded as a place for social training and the class teachers trained in multiple subjects are kept up to the end

---

3   Mainly run by conservative Christians.

of grade 7. The class teacher normally teaches RE but has the right to refuse. There are atheist, Muslim, humanist and Christian RE teachers. All teachers who attend general teacher training have religious studies as obligatory part of their training.[4] In lower secondary education subject teachers are more common.

In this state school, the only school subject where students were separated in different classrooms was Religious Education. To avoid this contradiction, the idea of a common multireligious school subject was and implemented in 1997 under the name of Christian Knowledge and Religious and Ethical Education.[5] The subject is normally referred to by the abbreviation KRL.[6]

Figure 1: The Norwegian school system

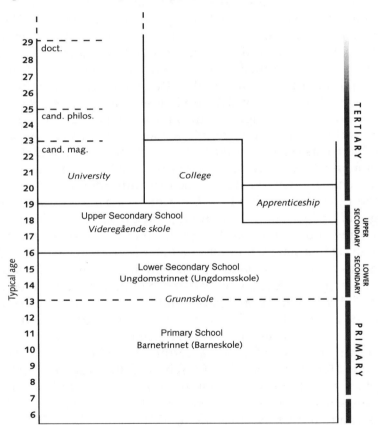

---

4   18,5 ECTS-credits in religious studies is minimum.
5   Literally: Knowledge of Christianity, Religions and World Views.
6   To the developmental process of the subject cf. Rasmussen, 2000.

A school subject for all

The general aim in curriculum development was to bring all students together when religious matters are discussed. The school was to work towards intercultural awareness, tolerance and respect. A prerequisite is knowledge of and insight into one's own religion, as well as that of others. The key words in the policy documents that launched the subject are *identity* and *dialogue* (NOU 1995:9). The teaching should support the development of individual identity and, at the same time, create space for dialogue and foster competence for dialogue across beliefs. Identity development depends on dialogue – and dialogue depends on a solid identity. The students are to gradually be trained in a dialogue that raises questions, awakens interest, and promotes understanding of the perspective of the other in ways that create new insight. One of the main aims for the subject is to promote the capacity for dialogue between people of different religions and beliefs (Utdanningsdirektoratet, 2005). Late modern plurality creates the need for an interreligious or meta-cultural competence even if the current plurality in Norwegian society is relatively limited. Young people live in an increasingly global world and need to develop the competence to live with diversity.

The subject was revised in 2002, after a comprehensive evaluation of school practices and after being discussed in Stortinget (Parliament), and in 2005. The first revision was to slim and simplify the subject and to improve the routines for information to secure the parental right.[7] A major concern for parents is to avoid confusion when it comes to the child's belonging, and the KRL-subject has undergone a revision process to strengthen the development of the individual child's identity. RE is supposed to gradually introduce the children to the plurality of religions, starting with the diversity present in the class and in the neighbourhood. The second revision was part of the Knowledge Promotion reform in 2006, in which all school curricula are being revised to be part of a competence based curriculum design. The basic approach is unchanged, equal treatment given to all the religions is emphasised, and the structure has made it easier to undertake comparisons and achieve dialogue between different religions and world views. The core curriculum of 1997 is a viable part of the latest educational reform. It encompasses the integral human being from six different aspects, starting with the spiritual.[8]

The common subject KRL is a regular school subject and grounded solely in educational considerations. It no longer means religious instruction or up-

---

7   Cf. British Journal of Religious Education 3/2006 for information of the outcomes of the evaluation (Hagesæther & Sandsmark, 2006).

8   The other five aspects are: the creative, the working, the liberally-educated, social and environmentally aware human being. http://www.skolenettet.no/templates/News.aspx?id=9022&scope=ScopeLaerAns&epslanguage=NO. The core curriculum is available in five languages.

bringing, and former links to the Church of Norway have been cut. A pre-condition for this RE-model is that religious nurture now is the responsibil-ity of families and religious communities. 'The intention of the subject KRL is to provide knowledge on various religions and outlooks on life, and not to teach any particular faith or creed' (Information letter to parents on KRL provided in 18 languages [KRL-book 2005:69-70]). 'The aim of the subject is to give insight into and impart knowledge of religions and outlooks on life in a qualitatively equal manner, without preaching or religious practice' (ibid). This means that the religions and world views are to be treated impartially and with methods that are appropriate to each religion, both on the particu-lar religion's premises and on a critical distance.

KRL – a compulsory subject

The need to keep all students together in a compulsory subject means that the subject only allows partial exemption. The right to opt out is limited to activities and there is no right to opt out of the purely content-related aspects of the subject. There have been severe conflicts about exemption rights in Norway.[9] The Norwegian Humanist Association and three families have ap-pealed to the European Court of Human Rights in Strasbourg. The plaintiffs lodged an appeal with the UN Human Rights Committee and the European Court of Human Rights. To act on the comments of the UN Human Rights Committee from the autumn of 2004, the subject of KRL and the rules in the Norwegian Education Act governing exemptions from the teaching was modified.

The exemption act applies to all school activities that generate the need for exemption for religious reasons.[10] This right does not apply specifically to KRL but to education in general:

> *The provisions on being excused from teaching in all subjects and joint schemes in school are given in the Education Act section 2-3a:*
> On the basis of written notification from parents, pupils shall be ex-empted from attending those parts of the teaching at the individual

---

9   The decision not to allow full exemption from the subject has led to sharp reactions both from individual parents, from religious communities and philosophical organisations. The Norwegian Humanist Association and the Islamic Council of Norway took legal action against the government during the period 1999-2001 for breach of religious freedom and parents' rights. The state was acquitted on all levels by the national courts. The courts found that the formal framework around the subject provides for a critical, neutral, objective and pluralistic form of teaching which neither preaches nor indoctrinates. It also determined that children have an autonomous right to learning and knowledge, independent of their parents' wishes.

10 Exemption has been treated as if it is a product of the school subject KRL. Religion affects schooling in a numerous of the school subjects, so the need for exemption cannot be limited to RE.

school that they, on the basis of their own religion or philosophy of life, perceive as being the practice of another religion or adherence to another philosophy of life, or which they for the same reasons find offensive or objectionable. It is not necessary to provide reasons for a notification of exemption pursuant to the first sentence. It is not possible to demand exemption from the knowledge content in the various syllabus topics. (…)

When the school receives a notification of exemption, it must ensure that the pupil in question is excused in actual practice, and facilitate for individually adapted and differentiated teaching within the scope of the syllabus.

Each year the school owner shall inform pupils and parents of pupils under 15 years of age about the exemption rules. Pupils who are 15 years of age or older may give written notification as stated in the first paragraph.

(Educational Act section 2-3a. In force as of 17 June 2005, KRL-2005-book:70)

This rule is used when pupils for religious reasons do not attend activities like: swimming lessons in gender mixed classes, lessons that involve handling pork, for instance in Home Economics, rhythmic pair dancing, overnight stays in gender mixed arrangements, movies or concerts, school services, Christmas preparations or birthday celebrations.

In KRL there are students that do not attend excursions to churches, mosques or temples if they assume or know some religious practice will be conducted, or if certain drama, singing, creeds, prayer, or artistic representations of holy persons will be part of the program.

'Schools must therefore exercise care when choosing how to work with the subject' (KRL-2005 book:69).[11] The overall impression is though that exemption is less used in KRL than in joint school activities such as Christmas preparations, school services and overnight stays.

The structure of KRL

The general aim for the subject is:

> *Educational Act Section 2-4. Teaching in the subject Christian Knowledge and Religious and Ethical Education:*
> Teaching in Christian Knowledge and Religious and Ethical Education shall
> – provide a thorough knowledge of the Bible and Christianity as cultural heritage
> – provide a thorough knowledge of the Lutheran Christianity and several Christian denominations

---

11 The evaluation of the implementation of KRL in 2000 showed that the number of parents requesting exemption for their children was about 1.5% (Hagesæther & Sandsmark, 2006).

- provide knowledge of world religions and world views
- provide knowledge of ethical and philosophical topics
- promote understanding and respect for Christian and humanist values and
- promote understanding, respect and the ability to carry out a dialogue between people with differing views concerning beliefs and world views.

The KRL subject is a regular school subject that normally enrols all pupils. The education is to take place without preaching. The teacher shall present Christianity, world religions, and world views from their own viewpoint. The same pedagogical principles shall be applied in all the various parts of the subject.

(In force as of 17 June 2005). (Lovdata, 1998)[12]

In primary education (grade 1-7) the total time for teaching is 427 hours (of 60 minutes) and at the lower secondary stage (grade 8-10) the total time for teaching is 157 hours. This gives an average of two lessons (of 45 minutes) per week. Each school may allocate the lessons as they find achieves the best learning result. The primary stage is divided in two and the achievement goals are structured by identifying the competence the students are supposed to have acquired at the end of the 4th grade and at the end of 7th grade. Here no formal evaluation in terms of grading takes place, only informal evaluation through comments, with marks only being used in the lower secondary stage. The subject can be chosen for formal exams at the end of the 10th grade, these being oral exams with preparation time. Learning results according to the new curriculum are expressed as competences which are defined as the ability to make use of the knowledge by articulating understanding of the various elements of the subject matter.

The teacher or the school has pedagogical freedom to develop their local curriculum from of the rather short and not too content-loaded national curriculum. The KRL-05 curriculum consists of 11 pages and is much less detailed than all earlier curricula (KRL-book, 2005). The subject is structured in three main fields:

Grade		Main Fields	
1-7	Christianity	Judaism, Islam, Hinduism, Buddhism, and World Views	Philosophy and Ethics
8-10	Christianity	Judaism, Islam, Hinduism, Buddhism, other religious diversity, and World Views	Philosophy and Ethics

---

12 Parts of the text have an official translation to English, parts are new and have been translated by the authors.

The teaching time allocated to the different areas should be: about 55% on Christianity, about 25% on Judaism, Islam, Hinduism, Buddhism, and World Views and about 20% on Philosophy and Ethics. All religions are identified by name, to signal their separate identity and to show that a systematic approach to them is preferred. On the other hand the plan is organised by addressing parallel themes in each of the religions to allow comparison, dialogue and thematic teaching. For instance, in grade 1-4 a personal perspective on each religion predominates, and religious practice in everyday life, prayer/meditation, celebrations of holy days, and art are parallel themes. At the higher stages, more advanced parallel themes are introduced. The area of Philosophy and Ethics also deals with comparison and dialogue between the different religions and world views and focuses on the relationship between faith and ethics.

The textbooks or the electronic learning resources are very important and strongly influence the choice of content. There was a thorough input process while developing textbooks in Norway. Each religious community was asked to comment on the presentation of their own faith. The religious communities are now given a voice in the curriculum development, but have no influence on the learning material.

2. Compulsory RE for all – an Example of Good Practice

In the following example a teaching project for 3rd grade pupils (8-9 year olds) is presented. The aim is to show how teaching can be carried out with a group of students and still be differentiated according to the students' background. The subjects included in the project are: KRL, Norwegian language, Art and Craft, Music and Science and Environmental Studies. Through KRL studies during this period of three weeks the students are to learn about birth rites in different religions and traditions. The students had twice the normal KRL lessons, which meant less time for KRL the next weeks.

Co-operation between school and home – differentiated teaching

When projects involve KRL it is important to inform parents and guardians of the program, to enable them to exercise the right to exemption when needed. Parents are also invited to take part in shaping the project. In this instance Mari's mother, who is a member of a Pentecostal congregation, suggests that we also make an excursion to their place of worship, Philadelphia, and look at the baptismal pool there. Mari's mother offers to arrange the visit and, at my[13] suggestion, agrees to tell the children about her beliefs concerning baptism. I know that she is a preschool teacher and a good narrator. Mari's

---

13   Refers to Elisabeth Haanes.

mother also suggests that we should get to know a couple of songs from the Pentecostal Christian tradition and provides us with the text and music.

The class consists of 21 children baptised into Church of Norway, two students who are secular humanists, one Muslim and one member of the Pentecostal movement. Espen's parents are members of the Humanist Association. They are concerned that he should be brought up as a citizen of the world and are critical of the large proportion of Christian material in KRL. They are positive about teaching about different faiths and world views. But this must be done neutrally, so that he has a suitable basis on which to develop his own interpretation. Espen is to be excused from learning by heart and reciting religious texts and he is not to join the singing of Christian hymns and songs when this occurs during teaching about religion.

Kristine's parents are also humanists. They are very critical about KRL as a subject. They would really prefer full exemption from all teaching about Christianity. Kristine is excused from various activities, including learning by heart, reciting or singing religious texts, taking part in religious dramatisations or church visits. When I present the planned project to them, they express satisfaction about the way different traditions are to be treated in parallel. Kristine herself wishes to take part in the excursions and her parents allow her.

Buskra's parents are Muslims. Buskra's mother attends the regular conferences about individual children twice a year, but not general parents' meetings. Her command of Norwegian is not very developed, but she refuses the offer to have an interpreter for the meeting. I have informed her about KRL, but cannot know how my message came through. Buskra's parents have not requested exemption from any of the activities in KRL and this troubles me. A more detailed discussion with Buskra's parents is needed, and I phone them to set up a home visit. I am warmly welcomed by the family and in the course of our conversation I get the information I need. Buskra may join the excursions, but she may not take part in any form of religious rituals there. She may certainly listen to hymns being sung, but may not join the singing herself. Buskra may draw nature, people and animals, but not God, angels or prophets.

To be able to offer a good and properly adjusted learning experience to each individual, all the pieces involved in specific exemption requirements must fall into place whilst the preparation work is being done.

Starting with 'myself' and my name

The teaching process itself started with the request to the students to ask the adults at home to tell them about when they were infants. They bring along pictures of themselves as babies, or an item (article of clothing, toy, doll etc.) as a reminder of their first year of life. All the students get to sit on the story chair and tell us about their own picture or object. This turns into a wonderful time every day where each individual has the attention and interest of all the others. As each one talks about her/himself, s/he ceremoniously hangs her/his picture or object on the wall. Science and Environmental Studies are brought in, so that the third-years can learn to be familiar with their own physical development and understand the human life cycle.

During ongoing work on the project we discuss what it means to give someone a name, the naming process and names in the family. Throughout a brainstorming session in class, I write up the students' suggestions of exciting things for further investigation. Each student decides individually what she or he will be working on and is placed in a group with corresponding plans. Some of them will be investigating which names are the most popular at school. Others are curious about how many of their forefathers had the same name as they have. With the help from the national register and the telephone directory Buskra finds another Buskra in Stavanger. Maria is curious about how many students in the school have biblical names like her own. The students admire the work of one another. During this period the students have been doing project work coming from their own questions.

Norwegian and Art and Craft are brought into play by getting the students to write their names as beautifully as they can in cursive script. Later, they experiment on the computer, and make simple clay stamps with their names on.

Different birth rituals – individual working plans

I ask if any of them know about celebrations or rituals connected with the naming of children. Espen mentions the name party he attended for his little brother. A similar party was given for him and they have many pictures of the day at home. Espen brings in some of these pictures to school. This fits this week's individual working plan. A working plan or weekly programme consists of tasks and activities in many subjects and fields. Everyone works within the framework of the same subject matter, but the amount, content and degree of difficulty are adjusted for the individual. Each student organises his own work schedule, depth of study and partners. Some tasks must be completed individually, whilst others require cooperation. The plans are adapted to match the qualifications, interests and faith background of the individual. The students are to investigate the practices of their own faith or world view in connection with birth. Everybody will present their findings in a plenary session.

When Espen presents the pictures from his name party, we get to know the background to the ceremony that was arranged by the Humanist Association. Kristine tells us about the name party for her cousin. She tells us she wore her national costume, which she uses for special occasions. Poems were read out and many fine songs were sung. Kristine brought along a CD with one of the songs. The students were familiar with the songs and could sing along.

Buskra finds out that there were also celebrations when she got her name. Buskra's parents help Buskra to prepare a short presentation of name giving, aqiqah, to the class. Nobody had heard of this celebration before.

Mari presented the blessing she had as a baby in the Pentecostal congregation and shows us the nice Children's Bible she has as a keepsake from that blessing.

The next day, the students are to learn about Christian baptism. Baptism is explained as a sacrament and not a naming ritual. Each child is blessed by its name. Colour transparencies of different baptismal fonts are shown and the biblical background of the sacrament is presented. The baptised children in the class tell us what they have found out about their baptism. Some have prepared short speeches, others show pictures. Five students act out the baptism ritual through a role-play they have prepared and practised. The baby is a doll.

During this part of the learning process each individual student acts as a resource person for the rest of the group. They show each other genuine interest and respect. The teacher mainly acts as a facilitator and tutor. The teaching is to bring together traditions, safeguard identities and build bridges that offer insight and promote communication.

Excursions

First we visit the local Lutheran church, which is within walking distance. The minister and organist are waiting for us in the sunshine. The children walk into the church two by two while the prelude sounds. The minister explains the Christian baptism ritual, and he allows the pupils time to ask him questions. Then the students have the opportunity to examine the font. The pupils are excited by the old font and the Christian symbols outlined in the stone. They recognise the Christogram on the christening candle and know what it means. The students know how to find their way through the hymn book and sing a couple of christening hymns that we studied beforehand. As the hymn singing fills the nave, the students exempted from the singing listen and study the christening hymn texts more closely.

Two days later we visit Philadelphia and the students meet a representative of another Christian denomination. Mari's mother, who is a Pentecostal Christian, receives us at the entrance and shows us around in the church. The children show great interest particularly in the baptismal pool. Mari's mother explains how baptism is practised in her congregation, and tells us about her own baptism. The children are given the opportunity to ask questions.

Achieving competence

The children have heard much about how birth rituals are celebrated and how newborn children are incorporated in the different faith communities. It will be interesting to see how they are able to put this knowledge to use. We make idea charts on the board. The children come up with words they associate with the project. Then each of them is asked to use some of these words and write a celebration song for a baptism, blessing, aqiqah or name party, depending on their individual faith or world view. Islam has no hymn tradition and religious songs play little part in the religion. Nonetheless Buskra will write a Muslim hymn. She gather in threads of Norwegian culture and weave them into her own. The self-composed hymns and songs will be illustrated. Not only Buskra decorates hers with stylised figures and ornaments. Islamic art has clearly inspired many to express themselves in the same way. Naturally all the students' work is signed with their own pottery stamps. Parents and other family members are invited to an exhibition, where they can get to see what the students have experienced and learned in the course of the project.

KRL – a balance of different expectations[14]

The project outlines an example of how a teacher can achieve a good balance between the needs of the society, the parents, the student group and the child by careful planning:

Society needs to communicate its values, traditions and inherited wisdom to new generations and to create common frames of reference in a modern world that is more complex and focused on the individual. Civic values are of the greatest importance and RE is expected to contribute to inculcating these values. The needs of the society do not always match with the wishes of the parents. This project allowed each child to deepen her/his heritage at the same time as they learned about one another. They learned to respect difference while the project traced common features between different faiths and world views when it comes to birth rituals and the importance of naming. The class shared experiences in the classroom and in important places of worship in the neighbourhood. They used this to encourage more mutual understanding, respect and tolerance. Thus, one teaches by going from the familiar to the unfamiliar, from the proximate to the distant.

Parents need to know that their child can develop a firm identity through confirmation of the values they bring to school. They want school and home to collaborate closely. This is a demanding task for the state school system.

---

14 The KRL-discussion is about how to strike the right balance between: The right of society, of the faith communities, of the parents, and of the child (Leirvik, 2002).

Good information and good co-operation between school and home is of the greatest importance when it comes to upbringing and values, and religious matters of central interest in this field. Trust minimises the need for exemptions. The school should seek solutions by arranging differentiated teaching within the framework of the curriculum. It must also be emphasised that differentiation in KRL should be concerned with differentiation of activity, not with differentiation of information. In the example given, the lessons were differentiated with regard to both activity and depth of study. The students worked on a common theme but approached it from their individual background. They took part in joint studies and acquired a common frame of reference through a mutual exchange of knowledge. All children came to know about Christian song traditions, but they did it by different means. In the case of Buskra we see how she met Christian hymns as both unfamiliar and strange, and ended up knowing them as familiar, though still strange – strangeness as a reflective distance – as she did not take part in the singing (Streib 2006). At the same time we see how cultural change happens. She transforms the hymns to her own tradition by inventing new Muslim songs.

The class in a way constitutes society on a small scale and is an arena for developing competence for life in the wider world. The class is a sheltered area, but still the conflicts and challenges within the group can be many and varied. The teacher's task is not to paper over or minimise the differences between the individuals in a classroom. They are necessary for the development of both individual identities and group cohesion. The respect the teacher and the school community show to religious affiliations is of great importance to achieve this end. Respect has to be practised and not just talked about. To live with difference is part of community building. A class or group needs a certain empathy and solidarity. These things are developed through a combination of shared experiences and room for individual contribution through the exchange of knowledge and experience. RE can easily be turned into a cognitively biased school subject where the teacher excludes activities that involve students and furnish enriching experiences in order to avoid the need for exemptions. Numerous styles of work and activities such as excursions, song and dance, artwork, role-play etc. help to bring the subject alive and make it interesting for the students. The students should be the active party for the most part, with the teacher acting as initiator, inspirer and guide. In the example presented, excursions, artwork and singing together can all take place even though there are exempt students in the class.

Each child has the right to information and education, independent of the needs and wishes of the parents. There must therefore be a limit to what the student can be exempted from. It is important for the teacher to safeguard this right in organising the lesson plan. In the example given, all students take part in the joint acquisition of knowledge. The challenge is to take account of all these considerations without making the subject boring, toothless and theoretical. In this case the students in the project work could shape their own questions and deepen their own interests. Competence for life in a multireligious and diverse world is achieved through dialogue developed in the classroom setting. An inclusive classroom in RE is therefore a good and safe place to start.

The example given highlights the central role of a sensitive and competent teacher who engages with both the subject and her students. A good teacher has the ability to inspire and enthuse.

3. Perspectives

In a state school system founded on the aims of equality and social cohesion like we have in Norway, RE in separate groups has more and more come to be seen as a contradiction. A compulsory subject for all was suggested and implemented. It was agreed that a limited right for exemption is necessary though this has given rise to a controversial debate. This has encouraged a lot of participation among parents and in communities. Upbringing, values and religion are matters of the greatest importance. There is considerable evidence that the debate on this profile of RE in a way anticipated developments in society. Now the subject is much more settled. According to empirical studies the students are very pleased and show a high level of interest in the subject (Hagesæther & Sandsmark, 2006). Religious diversity is an established fact and school plays an important role for children's life, allowing them to learn how to live together. The subject's intention is to systematically confirm and develop the individual identity of each student *and* develop dialogue and respect between students of different faiths and world views, as the case of Mustafa shows. KRL seeks to balance the needs of many stakeholders. There is a 'division of labour' between families, religious communities and schools. Nurture is mainly a task for the family and the religious communities, whereas the school mainly has an educational task. Curriculum development takes place at the national level, where the religious and philosophical communities have a say in the process. All general teachers are trained to do RE, and teaching materials are developed by educational publishers without input from religious communities. KRL emphasises 'learning about the religious approach' and prefers a systematic and holistic presentation of the different religions and world views.

References

Afdal, G., Haakedal, E., & Leganger-Krogstad, H. (Eds.) (2006 (1997)) *Tro, livstolkning og tradisjon: innføring i kontekstuell religionsdidaktikk. [Faith, life interpretation and tradition: introduction to a contextual approach to religious education]* (Oslo, Tano Aschehoug/Universitetsforlaget).

Birkedal, E., & Haanes, E. (2003) Enhet og mangfold i den offentlige skolen, [Unity and diversity in state school] in: T. Flateby (Ed.) *Tusenfryd. Skolefrihet og menneskeretter* (Oslo, Didakta), 141-150.

Hagesæther, G. & Sandsmark, S. (2006) Compulsory education in religion – the Norwegian case: an empirical evaluation of RE in Norwegian schools, with a focus on human rights, *British Journal of Religious Education*, 28 (3), 275-287.

Haanes, E. (2001) KRL-faget og tilpasset undervisning på småskoletrinnet, *[KRL and adapted teaching at the primary education level]* Prismet, 52 (1), 33-37.

Haanes, E. K. (2003) Røtter og vinger: religion og estetikk i grunnskolen *[Roots and wings. Religion and aesthetics in primary and lower secondary education]* (Oslo, IKO-forlaget).

Leganger-Krogstad, H. (1997) Religious Education in the Norwegian School System, in: R. E. Kristiansen & N. M. Terebichin (Eds.) *Religion, church and education in the Barents Region* (Arkhangelsk, Publishers of Pomor State University), 171-183.

Leganger-Krogstad, H. (2000) Developing a contextual theory and practice of Religious Education. *PANORAMA International Journal of Comparative Religions Education and Values*, 12 (1), 94-104.

Leganger-Krogstad, H. (2001) Religious Education in a Global Perspective: A Contextual Approach, in: H.-G. Heimbrock, C. T. Scheilke & P. Schreiner (Eds.) *Towards Religious Competence: Diversity as a Challenge for Education in Europe* (Münster/Hamburg/Berlin/London, LIT Verlag), 53-73.

Leganger-Krogstad, H. (2003) Dialogue among Young Citizens in a Pluralistic Religious Education Classroom, in: R. Jackson (Ed.) *International Perspectives on Citizenship, Education and Religious Diversity* (London, RoutledgeFalmer), 169-190.

Leirvik, O. (2002) *The current debate about religious education and freedom of religion in Norway.* Retrieved 07.10, 2006, from http://folk.uio.no/leirvik/OsloCoalition/Leirvik0902.htm

Lovdata. (1998) *Lov om grunnskolen og den vidaregåande opplæringa* (Opplæringslova). Retrieved 07.10.2006, from http://www.lovdata.no/all/tl-19980717-061-001.html

NOU 1995:9. (1995) *Official Norwegian Report: Identitet og dialog : kristendomskunnskap, livssyn-skunnskap og religionsundervisning [Identity and dialogue. Christian knowledge and religious and ethical education]* (Oslo, KUF).

Rasmussen, T. (2000) The New Norwegian 'KRL' Subject and Religious Freedom: a Report, *Studia Theologica*, 54 (1), 19-34.

Skeie, G. (2006) Diversity and the political function of religious education, *British Journal of Religious Education*, 28 (1), 19-32.

Streib, H. (2006) Strangeness in Inter-Religious Classroom Communication: Research on the 'Gift-to-the-Child' Material, in: D. Bates, G. Durka & F. Schweitzer (Eds.) *Religion, Reconciliation and Inclusion in a Pluralistic World.* Essays in Religious Education and Practical Theology in Honour of John M. Hull (London/New York, Routledge) 191-204.

Utdanningsdirektoratet (2005) KRL-boka 2005 : Kristendoms-, religions- og livssynskunnskap, læreplan for 1.-10. årstrinn, læreplanveiledning og informasjon, from http://www.krl-nett.no/innhold/krkbok/lareplan.pdf

Contributors

Dr. Bojidar Andonov, Lecturer in Religious Education at the Theological Faculty in Sofia, doctorate at the Theological Faculty of the Catholic University in Eichstätt/Germany, Prof. Dr. Engelbert Groß). Member of the Committee for Religious Education of the Ministry of Education, member of the diocese of central Europe of the Bulgarian-Orthodox Church.

Derek Bastide is Principal Lecturer and Faculty Co-coordinator of Schools Liaison at the University of Brighton/England.

Dr. Petra Freudenberger-Lötz, Education Philosopher, Primary and Secondary school teacher, Lecturer in Theology and Religious Education at the University of Education in Karlsruhe/Germany.

Prof. Dr. Helmar-Ekkehart Pollitt is Director of the Institute for Religious Education of the Protestant Church of Austria.

Dipl. Päd. Gerhild Herrgesell, teaches Protestant RE since 1983 in all types and levels of schools, since 10 years specialised for secondary I level. She teaches also at the Protestant RE Academy and at the teacher training seminar Didactics of secondary I level. For many years active church member, since 2006 deputy regional trustee.

Elisabeth Kvadsheim Haanes has been a teacher in the Norwegian primary school for 25 years, worked as a consultant in the Church Education Centre in Oslo, lecturing Didactics at MF Norwegian School of Theology and in several University Colleges. She has been a committee-member in the Norwegian Government Commission on Human Values, working with National Tests and a member of the Governmental Curriculum Commission. She is the author of 'Røtter og vinger. Religion og estetikk i grunnskolen' (2003) (Religion and Aesthetics in Primary School).

Prof. Dr. Friedhelm Kraft is Director of the RE Centre of the Protestant-Lutheran Church of Hanover in Loccum/Germany. He has set up a 'network of child theology' with colleagues from Germany, Austria and the Netherlands.

Heid Leganger-Krogstad, Associate Professor in Philosophy of Religious Education at MF Norwegian School of Theology, Oslo/Norway.

Dr. Henk Kuindersma is Lecturer in Religious Education at the Protestant University in Kampen. He is a member of the research group on religion in the life cycle; in this group he gives special attention to children.

Juha Luodeslampi is Senior Lecturer at the Institute for Religious Education in Finland. The institute is developing methods and producing material and training for RE teachers in service. He is working in close co-operation with the department of Applied Sciences of Education at the University of Helsinki.

Maria Luisa Mazzarello is a Lecturer in Catechetics (chatechetica) at the Pontificia Facoltá di Scienze dell' Educazione 'Auxilium' in Rome (papal faculty for education philosophy).

James Nelson is a Lecturer in Religious Studies and Religious Education at Stranmillis University College Belfast (Northern Ireland) and an experienced author of school textbooks for religious education. James also currently leads the Good Practice in Diverse Schools (GoPIDS) project, which facilitates inter-school collaboration for teachers and visits for student-teachers to schools of different ethos and management-type in Northern Ireland.

Sari Nevalainen is a theologian and a Primary school teacher. She works as a Lecturer at the Institute for Religious Education in Finland. Her main task is to support primary teachers in RE by making materials and organising in service training for them.

Olga Schihalejev has been co-writer of teaching-learning resources for Religious Education of all school stages; teaches religious education, personal and social development at Carl Robert Jakobson's Gymnasium in Viljandi. Currently she is a doctoral student at Tartu University, Faculty of Theology and is a Lecturer at the Institute of Theology of the Estonian Evangelical Lutheran Church.

Peter Schreiner is Educational Researcher at the Comenius-Institut, Protestant Centre for Research and Development in Education, Münster/Germany, President of the Intereuropean Commission on Church and School.

Dr. Pille Valk, is historian and theologian, Senior Lecturer in Religious Education at the University of Tartu/Estonia and Lecturer at the University of Helsinki/Finland.

Drs. Johan G. Valstar is Senior Lecturer in Religious Education at the Windesheim School of Education In Zwolle. He is doing research on the field of new media and e-learning environments. At the moment his main research topic is the conceptual development of religious education within the framework of teacher education.

Dr. Andrew Wright is Senior Lecturer in Religious and Theological Education at King's College, London/England.

Schriften aus dem Comenius-Institut
hrsg. von Volker Elsenbast (Münster)

Christoph Th. Scheilke
Von Religion lernen heute
Befunde und Perspektiven in Schule, Gemeinde und Kirche
Bd. 6, 2003, 344 S., 35,90 €, br., ISBN 3-8258-7332-3

Peter Biehl; Karl Ernst Nipkow
Bildung und Bildungspolitik in theologischer Perspektive
Woran ist Bildung in evangelischer Perspektive theologisch zu erkennen? Wie wird Bildung im öffentlichen Bildungsdiskurs und in der Bildungspraxis wirksam? Peter Biehl stellt die Wiederentdeckung der Bildung in der gegenwärtigen Religionspädagogik dar, fundiert Bildung ausführlich theologisch im Gespräch mit der Systematischen Theologie und entfaltet den Bildungsbegriff als religionspädagogische Grundkategorie mit Bezug zur Pädagogik. Karl Ernst Nipkow rückt das Thema in den gesellschaftlichen und politischen Raum und zeigt, wie Bildung und evangelische Bildungspolitik historisch-systematisch zusammenhängen. Er erläutert die kürzlich veröffentlichte Bildungsdenkschrift des Rates der Evangelischen Kirche in Deutschland (EKD) „Maße des Menschlichen". Das Buch kommentiert damit als erstes die neueste Entwicklung mit Blick auf die Zukunft.
Bd. 7, 2. Aufl. 2005, 280 S., 19,90 €, br.,
ISBN 3-8258-6558-4

Gert Rüppell; Peter Schreiner (eds.)
Shared Learning in a Plural World
Ecumenical Approaches to Inter-Religious Education
"Shared Learning in a Plural World" takes the reader along to a discourse held between representatives of different World Religions, religious educators and researchers about "How religious education can contribute to good community relations." Starting with the issue of pluralism, the book leads on to concepts of learning in world religions, reflections on inter-religious learning in Europe, and examples on methodologies of education and community. A number of documents related to the Interfaith work of the World Council of Churches are also documented. The publication is an outcome of a co-operation between the World Council of Churches (Education and Ecumenical Formation / Inter-religious Relations) and the Comenius-Institut in Münster, Germany.
Bd. 8, 2003, 184 S., 19,90 €, br., ISBN 3-8258-6571-1

Heide Liebold
Religions- und Ethiklehrkräfte in Ostdeutschland
Eine empirische Studie zum beruflichen Selbstverständnis
Wie stellen sich die Fächer Evangelische Religion und Ethik aus der Sicht ostdeutscher Unterrichtender dar? Die Studie nimmt die Motivation der Lehrkräfte für die Übernahme des neuen Faches, die im Unterricht verfolgten Ziele, aber auch die mit beiden Fächern verbundenen Probleme sowie Möglichkeiten der fächerübergreifenden Kooperation in den Blick. Exemplarische Fallstudien geben einen Einblick in typische Formen berufsbiografischer Orientierung. Die Diskussion der Ergebnisse führt zu Impulsen für die Aus-, Weiter- und Fortbildung von Religions- und Ethiklehrkräften. Die 48 Interviews als empirische Basis der Studie sind auf CD-ROM dokumentiert.
Bd. 9, 2004, 288 S., 19,90 €, br., ISBN 3-8258-7123-1

Klaus Ziller
Gemeinsame Verantwortung der evangelischen und katholischen Kirche für den Religionsunterricht in Ostdeutschland
Eine Untersuchung aus evangelischer Perspektive anhand religionspädagogischer und kirchlicher Stellungnahmen und evangelischer und katholischer Lehrpläne
Die vorliegende Untersuchung reflektiert auf theologischer, pädagogisch-didaktischer, inhaltlicher und schulorganisatorischer Ebene nach der Frage nach angemessenen und zukunftsfähigen Formen des Religionsunterrichts in den ostdeutschen Bundesländern. Ausgehend von den Rahmenbedingungen des Religionsunterrichts, kirchlichen Stellungnahmen und den derzeit geltenden Lehrplänen entwirft sie Ansatzpunkte für eine Neukonzeption des Religionsunterrichts, die dem spezifischen ostdeutschen Kontext Rechnung tragen. Die speziellen Rahmenbedingungen des Religionsunterrichts legen auch die verstärkte Kooperation der evangelischen und katholischen Kirche im Religionsunterricht im Sinne „gemeinsamer Verantwortung" für die Schülerinnen und Schüler in ihren konkreten Lebenssituationen nahe.
Bd. 10, 2004, 272 S., 19,90 €, br., ISBN 3-8258-7416-8

Nicole Piroth
Gemeindepädagogische Möglichkeitsräume biographischen Lernens
Eine empirische Studie zur Rolle der Gemeindepädagogik im Lebenslauf
Gegenstand dieser Studie sind die Möglichkeiten, die die gemeindepädagogischen Handlungsfelder

LIT Verlag Berlin – Hamburg – London – Münster – Wien – Zürich
Fresnostr. 2 48159 Münster
Tel.: 0251 – 62 032 22 – Fax: 0251 – 23 19 72
e-Mail: vertrieb@lit-verlag.de – http://www.lit-verlag.de

der evangelischen Kirche unter heutigen gesellschaftlichen Bedingungen für biographische Lern- und Bildungsprozesse im Erwachsenenalter bereitstellen. Hierzu wurden in einer empirischen Studie 22 Menschen interviewt. Aus der Perspektive der Nutzer/innen wird gefragt, welche Möglichkeiten biographischen Lernens in der Lebensspanne gemeindepädagogische Arrangements bieten, wie sich dies auf das Verhältnis zur Institution Kirche auswirkt und wie die Professionalität der Gemeindepädagogen und -pädagoginnen – im Unterschied zu Pfarrern und Sozialpädagogen – wahrgenommen wird.

Bd. 11, 2004, 328 S., 24,90 €, br., ISBN 3-8258-7818-x

Ulrich Becker
Hoffnung für die Kinder dieser Erde
Beiträge für Religionspädagogik und Ökumene. Herausgegeben von Gottfried Orth
„Das Kind in die Mitte stellen?" – darum geht es in dem weit verzweigten Werk des Hannoveraner Religionspädagogen, evangelischen Theologen und Ökumenikers Prof. Dr. Ulrich Becker. Der Band versammelt religionspädagogische, systematisch-theologische und ökumenewissenschaftliche Aufsätze aus Beckers unterschiedlichen Arbeitsgebieten, deren einigendes Band seine ökumenische und religionspädagogische Sorge um die Kinder dieser Erde ist. Es finden sich Beiträge zu Religionsunterricht und Schule, Kirche und Bildung, zu ökumenischen Themen und zu dem Lebensthema Ulrich Beckers: zum ökumenischen Lernen. Eine komplette Bibliographie der Publikationen Beckers erschließt dessen Arbeit für die weitere theologische Forschung. Der Band dokumentiert so ein Stück Geschichte der Religionspädagogik, der Ökumene und der Theologie in Deutschland und weit darüber hinaus!

Bd. 12, 2004, 336 S., 19,90 €, br., ISBN 3-8258-7954-2

Martin Rothgangel; Dietlind Fischer (Hg.)
Standards für religiöse Bildung?
Zur Reformdiskussion in Schule und Lehrerbildung
Im Rahmen der jüngsten bildungspolitischen Reformbemühungen geraten auch Verantwortliche für den Religionsunterricht zusehends unter Druck, Standards für religiöse Bildung zu formulieren. Die Ambivalenz dieser Thematik verlangt nach gründlicher Auseinandersetzung. Der vorliegende Band stellt eine religionspädagogische Zwischenbilanz der Debatte um religiöse Standards und Kompetenzen dar und zeigt Facetten der Problematik aus ganz unterschiedlichen Perspektiven auf.

Bd. 13, 2., durchges. Aufl. 2005, 248 S., 19,90 €, br., ISBN 3-8258-8135-0

Joachim Willems
Religiöse Bildung in Russlands Schulen
Orthodoxie, nationale Identität und die Positionalität des Faches „Grundlagen orthodoxer Kultur" (OPK)
Die Diskussion um die Einführung von Schulfächern, die Religion thematisieren, ist in Russland kontrovers: Einerseits erwarten viele von der Schule einen Beitrag zur religiösen Renaissance im Lande. Andererseits wird befürchtet, dass das orthodoxe Christentum zur neuen Staatsideologie werden könnte. Die vorliegende Untersuchung analysiert in diesem Zusammenhang das umstrittene Fach „Grundlagen orthodoxer Kultur", in dem sich eine Einführung in orthodoxe Sichtweisen mit staatsbürgerkundlichen und moralerziehenden Elementen verbindet. Weitere Beiträge zur Sichtweise religiöser Minderheiten zur religiösen Bildung in den Schulen, zur Einführung religionsorientierter Fächer in verschiedenen Regionen Russlands sowie Analysen zu russischer Rockmusik ergänzen den Band.

Bd. 14, 2006, 216 S., 19,90 €, br., ISBN 3-8258-9345-6

Meinolf Schultebraucks
Behindert leben
Lebensgeschichten körperbehinderter Menschen als Leitmotive subjektverbundener Theologie und Pädagogik. Mit einem Vorwort von J. B. Metz
Ausgehend von zwei Interviewserien aus den Jahren 1982 und 2002 werden in der biographieanalytischen Studie Lebenssituationen, Selbstkonzepte und Bewältigungsstrategien von drei körperbehinderten Erwachsenen beschrieben. Gemeinsames Merkmal ist die auffällig positive Grundhaltung der Autobiographen zum eigenen Leben, die im krassen Widerspruch zur gesellschaftlich vorgenommenen Einschätzung der Lebensqualität von behinderten Menschen als gering oder Mitleid erregend steht. Als weiteres durchgängiges Kennzeichen der untersuchten Biographien stellte sich das Bemühen um die Herstellung von Normalität heraus. „... die Überlegungen des Verfassers (zielen) auf gesteigerte gesellschaftliche Partizipation von Behinderten, die schließlich zu einer gesamtgesellschaftlichen Veränderung ihrer Situation und der Art ihres Lebens beitragen soll" (Johann Baptist Metz).

Bd. 16, 2006, 304 S., 19,90 €, br., ISBN 3-8258-9429-0

LIT Verlag Berlin – Hamburg – London – Münster – Wien – Zürich
Fresnostr. 2 48159 Münster
Tel.: 0251 – 62 032 22 – Fax: 0251 – 23 19 72
e-Mail: vertrieb@lit-verlag.de – http://www.lit-verlag.de